MIND POWER

MIND POWER

Picture Your Way to Success in Business

Gini Graham Scott, Ph.D.

PARKER PUBLISHING COMPANY
West Nyack, New York 10995

Prentice-Hall International, Inc., *London*
Prentice-Hall of Australia, Pty. Ltd., *Sydney*
Prentice-Hall Canada, Inc., *Toronto*
Prentice-Hall of India Private Ltd., *New Delhi*
Prentice-Hall of Japan, Inc., *Tokyo*
Prentice-Hall of Southeast Asia Pte. Ltd., *Singapore*
Editora Prentice-Hall do Brasil Ltda., *Rio de Janeiro*
Prentice-Hall Hispanoamericana, S.A., *Mexico*

© 1987 by

Gini Graham Scott, Ph.D.

10 9 8 7 6 5

Library of Congress Cataloging-in-Publication Data

Scott, Gini Graham.
  Mind power

  Includes index.
  1. Success in business.   2. Mental discipline.
I. Title.
HF5386.S413 1987   650.1   87-6923

ISBN 0-13-583527-5

ISBN 0-13-583519-4 {PBK}

About the Author

Gini Graham Scott, Ph.D., is a marketing and management consultant, published writer, speaker, and seminar/workshop leader specializing in creativity, direct sales, and small business practices.

She is the founder and president of Creative Communications and Research and Marketing Specialists and has had over eighteen years experience in marketing, market research, and writing books and training materials. Additionally, as a game designer and consultant, she has had over two dozen games on the market with major companies, including Hasbro Industries, Pressman Toy, and Mag-Nif. A new toy company will be bringing out five lines of dolls and children's books she developed in 1987.

Dr. Scott has a Ph.D. in Sociology from the University of California at Berkeley. She is currently attending law school at the University of San Francisco.

Aside from *Mind Power! Picture Your Way to Success in Business*, Dr. Scott has authored five other business books: *Effective Selling and Sales Management* published by Brick House, *Strike it Rich in Personal Selling* published by Avon Books, *Debt Collection: Successful Strategies for the Small Business* published by Oasis Press, *How to Collect a Judgment in California* published by Nolo Press, and *It's Your Money: How to Collect What People Owe You*, a mass-market paperback published by Avon.

Dr. Scott has also had articles on marketing, creativity, and mind power techniques published in major trade publications, and she hosted one of the first shows in the United States dealing with direct sales (*Make Money with MLM* broadcast in San Francisco).

Recently, she has been a featured speaker for numerous trade shows, distributor organizations, and direct sales companies all over the country. She has been a guest on national talk shows, including the Phil Donahue Show, the Sally Jessy Raphael Show, and other talk shows in New York, Los Angeles, Chicago, and San Francisco.

CONTENTS

Introduction

The dynamic mind power techniques you will learn in this book are designed to help you succeed and get what you want, particularly in your work or business.

These techniques are based on abilities all of us have within us, but that are often unused or not fully developed. This book will show you how to tap into these powers, so you can function more productively, efficiently, creatively, and happily in work and other settings.

I wrote this book after working with these techniques for over fifteen years and using them constantly for business and everyday situations. For example, I used them to write eight published books in less than three years; to get over twenty-four games on the market with different companies; to up my income from an average of $2,000 to 3,000 to nearly $8,000 in one month; to make business decisions about hiring people and selecting projects to work on; and to adapt to changing circumstances. I have also been conducting workshops on this topic.

I felt if these techniques worked so well for me in helping me become successful and making my life run more smoothly, then others could benefit, too.

HOW THESE TECHNIQUES CAN BENEFIT YOU

You'll find these powerful life-changing techniques can increase your success dramatically. Here are just some of the ways these techniques can help you.

Overcome stress and relax. In today's high-paced, competitive world, stress is extremely common. A little stress can be stimulating, but too much interferes with your performance and your satisfaction. With these techniques, though, you can immediately reduce feelings of pressure and learn to confront tense situations, like a job interview, sales presentation, or negotiation session, with more comfort and ease.

Raise your energy and overcome fatigue. Everyone needs an extra energy boost at times. You may have a deadline to meet and need to work around the clock. You may not feel in the mood to participate in an important meeting. You may need to appear on top of things in the office after a long weekend that went on for too long. These techniques can give you just the boost you need to feel and appear energized.

Feel more confident, self-assured, and have higher self-esteem. Feeling confident is a key to success, and the more you succeed, the more confidence, self-assurance, and self-esteem you will feel. In turn, as your confidence rating goes up, the more likely you are to get the job, promotion, account, relationship, or anything you want. By using these techniques, you become more certain of achieving what you want, feel more capable to obtain it, are more sure you deserve it, and thus feel more convinced you can do it, and so you will!

Set goals and attain them. You have to know what you want to get it, and you have to work out a realistic series of steps to achieve this end. Whether your goals involve work, relationships, personal development, material objects you want, or whatever, the process is the same. These techniques can help you set your goals, increase the abilities you need to get them, and motivate you to act at once to get what you want. For example, you can increase your income and improve your life style by using these mind power techniques to change your attitudes about yourself, set new goals, and be open to opportunities.

Increase your skills and creativity. The better you are at what you do, the more you'll move ahead. These techniques can be applied to improving any skill you want to develop—be it sales ability, typing, being more organized, speaking better, or whatever. Also, use these techniques to become more creative and innovative, so you are in a better position to be successful in these rapidly changing, challenging times. Improve your memory, too!

Create the personality and self-image you want. To achieve a desired goal, you may need to make some personal changes in yourself or in the image you present. For instance, to get a desired promotion, you need to begin looking and carrying yourself in a way that suits the new job you want. To create a more satisfying relationship with work associates or employees, you need to better understand what they need and expect from you, and change your attitudes and actions accordingly. These mind power techniques will help you recognize the changes you must make and help you take the necessary steps to effect these changes.

Gain insight into others so you can improve your relationships and be more persuasive in motivating others. A key to working successfully with others or to managing an organization is understanding others. This understanding can also help you recognize what others need and want, so you can motivate them to act. These mind power techniques can give you the insight you need to do this. In turn, the benefits to you from improved relationships and a greater ability to be persuasive are countless—more personal satisfaction, further career advancement, more sales, more of whatever you want.

Solve problems and make decisions. The further you advance, the more responsibilities you assume, and, the more you need to be able to solve problems and make decisions. Problem-solving and decision-making are the tools of good managers—and the quicker they can resolve matters, the more productive and efficient they can be. These techniques help you in this area by giving you insight and helping you approach the task in a more relaxed, confident, and stressfree way.

Improve your health and eliminate bad habits. Do you want to lose weight? Stop smoking? Reduce anxiety? Get rid of headaches? Overcome illnesses? Feel better generally? You'll be more productive, efficient, creative, and happy if you can do these things, for better health and habits contribute to your success at work and in other areas of life, as well. These techniques will help you achieve better health and habits, so you can better get what you want.

In short, there are numerous things you can do to create a more favorable situation for yourself and achieve your goals. You can do this because you affect what happens to you by your own outlook and system of beliefs; you shape the world you experience. Thus, when you use these techniques, you learn to be more aware of opportunities and are more ready to take advantage of them. Also, you will find the number of favorable "coincidences" in your life increasing, too!

Call it luck; call it ESP; call it "mind power"—whatever you call it, you'll notice your work life and other parts of your life changing for the better when you use these techniques.

 *Chapter 1*

The Dynamics of Mind Power Techniques

HOW THESE TECHNIQUES WORK

These mind power techniques work because they get you more in touch with your intuition, inner voice, true self, powers of creative visualization, inner knowing, or whatever you want to call this. It's a very powerful force within you.

Often this force is covered up or downplayed in modern society, because of the emphasis on being rational, solving problems, making decisions, and working out situations logically. For example, lawyers, judges, business people, scientists, engineers, politicians—essentially, most of the leaders of our society—are praised and rated for their ability to reach reasoned decisions. And the rationalism of the computer and high technology is the watchword of our age.

Yet, we all have open to us this intuitive, nonrational side, which harnessed and used properly can help us function more effectively in business and in other settings.

Recently, research has linked these intuitive functions with the operations of the right hemisphere of the brain, which has a holistic mode of perceiving information, whereas the left hemisphere uses a logical, linear mode to reason things out. This holistic style is associated with creativity, visual imagery, dreams, feelings, symbols, and

1

synthesis, in contrast to the more linear style associated with mathematics, writing, language, and analysis.

Initially, children use this holistic mode of thinking. At first, they see the world in terms of images, feelings, and sensations. But as they learn language, they are taught to discount their immediate intuitive responses and to favor a more analytical rational approach to the world.

Developing these reasoning abilities is, of course, very necessary. The problem comes in repressing the natural intuition at the same time. Thus, these mind power techniques are designed to release and develop this inner force within us, which has an incredible power to help us gain all of the benefits previously described, which include:

- overcome stress and relax
- raise your energy and overcome fatigue
- feel more confident, self-assured, and have higher self-esteem
- set goals and attain them
- increase your skills and creativity
- create the personality and self-image you want
- gain insight into others to improve relationships and be more persuasive in motivating others
- solve problems and make decisions
- improve your health and eliminate bad habits

This inner force helps us attain these benefits, as it operates powerfully in two main modes:

- *a receptive mode,* that helps to give us insight, information, and understanding, which we don't pick up rationally. In turn, we can use this information to make more informed decisions, recognize problems, establish goals and priorities, and better assess the people we work with or contact in everyday life.
- *an active mode,* that acts, based on the information we have, to shape ourselves, influence others, and affect events.

While some mind power techniques emphasize one mode or the other, most involve some combination of the two approaches. For example, when you use these techniques to set goals, you will first use your receptive powers to gain insights about what you want and need. Then, based on these insights, you can establish your goals, prioritize them, and set up a system for achieving what you want.

You can tap into this receptivity and ability to act on insights through your power to perceive intuitively. Commonly, this intuitive perception operates through your ability to create images, visualizations, or pictures in your head—a skill that everyone possesses or can develop to some degree. But some people will prefer to tune in to this inner voice by listening to the words or their inner thoughts. Others will tend to respond more to feelings or sensations.

However, as the visual and auditory modes of perception are most common, the techniques described in this book draw more heavily on the ability to use images or thoughts to tap this power of the mind. In turn, as you work with these techniques, you'll develop these abilities.

THE EFFECTIVENESS OF THESE TECHNIQUES— SOME EXAMPLES

The benefits of these techniques can best be illustrated by showing some examples of what people have gained by using them. This will give you an idea of how much you can gain by using these techniques.

For example, Ann S., a teacher in her thirties, who operated a small secretarial business in her home, was able to relocate her business quickly and efficiently when her landlord told her she would have to move, because the landlord wanted to move in. At the time the landlord made this decision, Ann had no plans to move, and she also lived in a city with an extremely low vacancy rate. Yet within a few days, with minimal effort, she found a more ideal situation using these techniques.

How did she do it? First, she did not worry about the move. She felt certain she had the power to find a good place and to do so in an efficient way. Also, she did not struggle against what was a *fait accompli* or feel upset about the potential disruption to her life. Instead, she accepted the event and was determined to do what she could to turn this into a creative change that could actually benefit her business.

To do this, she began imagining the possibilities. She got relaxed and let mental pictures form in her head as she asked herself a series of questions. She did not try to get the answers logically. Instead, she was receptive to the pictures or images that appeared.

Some of the questions she asked were: Where would I like to see my business going in the next two years? What would I like to be doing? Where would it be best to do these activities? What kind of place will I need? How many rooms do I want? How much can I pay?

Eventually, she had a clear picture of exactly what she wanted and a specific area of the city where she wanted it. Then, using a rational mode of thinking, she collected the appropriate information. For example, she drove up and down the streets in the area where she wanted to live looking for "For Sale" or "For Rent" signs, so she could collect the names and phone numbers of the owners or real estate agents handling property in the area. Then, listening to her inner voice again, she determined the best time to start looking, and when the timing was right, she began calling the owners and agents, as well as looking through the paper.

As she talked to people on the phone, she actively pictured the places they described and got a feeling of what it would be like to live and work there. As she already knew what she wanted, her receptive listening involved fitting the picture of the place described with the image she already had in her mind.

As a result, after about an hour of phone calls and four hours of looking, she had located a place that seemed ideal and had just been placed on the market. She arranged to meet with the owner and after a few minutes, she was convinced that this was the place and there was no need to look any further. She conveyed this certainty to the owner, put down a deposit, and in a few days was given a lease—for exactly the time she wanted to move. The whole process had taken only a few hours of looking at a handful of places.

In another case, Tom R. used these mind power techniques to increase his sales income. He had been averaging about $25,000 a year in various sales jobs, ranging from selling health products to marketing gift items. Then he began using some visualization techniques to see himself getting a larger monthly income. He began by focusing on getting another $4,000 a month. He visualized himself very clearly receiving the additional money and being congratulated for doing the job well by his supervisor. He concentrated on what he would have to do to achieve this goal, and he imagined the steps in his mind. Also, with the new confidence he gained at seeing his goal completed, he felt more motivated to act and was much more enthusiastic than he had ever been.

Thus, when he approached prospects, he exuded an air of self-assurance that was contagious. His contacts responded by having more confidence in the product he was selling and his orders increased. Also, the cold calls he made by phone resulted in more people who wanted to see him and learn about his product, so that increased his orders, too. In addition, he was more receptive to everyday opportunities to talk about his product with enthusiasm, which increased sales figures as well. As a result, he made close to $5,000 that month, and given that success, he started the next month with $5,000 as his sales goal, and he felt confident of making that amount.

Similarly, Mary J. improved her relationship with her boss, who was frequently critical of her performance, by focusing on having a better relationship. She used the mind power techniques to get insights into her boss's personality and needs so she could relate to him better. She increased her own skills in the areas where her boss had been critical by mentally concentrating on improving these abilities—typing more accurately and following-up better on phone calls. She changed her own attitude, so she was more positive and receptive when her boss made suggestions. Thus she wasn't so defensive about what she had done and instead showed a willingness to improve. Additionally, she exuded a new confidence and certainty she would succeed that showed up in her walk and the way she stood, so she had an increased presence in the office. Everyone could feel her new sense of calm assurance. The result after two months: a promotion to administrative assistant, increased responsibilities, and a substantial raise.

Other people, whom you'll read about in subsequent chapters, show similar successes. In turn, as you read these stories, you'll better understand how you can use these high-power techniques to improve your own way of functioning at work and in other areas of your life.

These methods are something anyone can master. They're not mysterious or magic. They're based on sound psychological principles describing how the intuitive right-brained power within you operates, so you function more effectively and can better create the reality you want.

THE DEVELOPMENT OF THESE TECHNIQUES

I have been developing and using these techniques for over fifteen years, so that now they have become so much a part of my life that I don't even think about them. I just do them.

I first started using them in 1968 when I began designing games. I used the pictures in my mind to develop game ideas. I imagined myself going into Macy's toy department, where I saw all sorts of new games and immediately knew the rules to them. I created hundreds of games this way and got about two dozen of them on the market—a phenomenal result, given the competitiveness of the games industry.

Eventually, I no longer needed to go to this imaginary toy store or go through any preparatory techniques to see pictures of games in my mind. I would simply see the game ideas and people playing them in my imagination in an instant—and I found I could use this instant awareness approach on other creative projects.

Besides my own experiments with these methods, I went to dozens of workshops on developing creativity, working with hypnosis, using visualization and imagery, meditating, and the like—all designed to expand the power of the mind.

Then, when I went for my doctorate in sociology at the University of California at Berkeley, where I specialized in the study of groups, I found that the spiritual and personal growth groups I studied also used some of these same techniques to further self-development. Later, when I worked in other fields—program evaluation, marketing new products, creating and motivating a sales team—I automatically used these techniques to come up with ideas and make decisions. Also, I readily applied them in other areas of my life to solve problems, relax, improve relationships, become a better speaker, give better presentations—just about everything I do. Most recently, I have used them to create a job for myself as a national marketing director for a major travel company, to create a line of dolls now being marketed by a national doll company, and to write eight books that have been published.

The mind power techniques described in this book represent the methods I have found effective in tapping this inner force. You can use the same methods or feel free to adapt them by changing the imagery to suit your own style. For instance, use a computer screen instead of a movie screen to see mental images; use a female counselor instead of a male one to get information and advice.

The key to success with these techniques is to use a series of procedures and symbols to make yourself *receptive* to contacting this inner force within you. Then, once you are in contact, *actively mobilize* this force to achieve your desired goals.

 *Chapter 2*

Preparing to Use the Mind Power Techniques

Using these mind power techniques will eventually become second nature, and you may not need any preparatory methods to activate them. Initially, though, you must set the stage in order to trigger the appropriate receptive or active mode. Then, after you have gone through enough "set constructions" and "rehearsals," these techniques will be ready to perform when you want them.

There are four key steps to getting properly prepared.

1. Be aware of how your own mind powers operate, so you can get more information and insights from these techniques.
2. Schedule some regular time each day to practice.
3. Choose a good setting for your practice.
4. Get relaxed when you begin using a method that is comfortable for you.

In addition, it is helpful to have a notebook or tape recorder to record your ideas and insights.

KNOWING YOUR OWN MIND

Recognizing how your mind powers operate will help you know when to trust and act on your insights from these techniques. This is the case

7

because everyone's mind powers work differently. Some people are more visually oriented, so they take in most of their information by seeing pictures. Others are more auditory and take in information primarily by words or thoughts. Still others get strong feelings or sensations, or have a sense of "knowing" something is correct.

We all have abilities in these four areas, although to varying degrees. Furthermore, we can improve our powers in each area by working with them.

Thus, you will probably find your ability to see and listen increased as you use the techniques in this book. However, to use these methods most effectively, first judge where you are now, so you know where you want to develop and can better assess the knowledge and ideas you get through these techniques. Then you can decide when and how to act appropriately.

The following two techniques will give you this insight.

1. Getting in Touch with Your Mind Powers

To learn how you receive information, try this exercise. Close your eyes and think of the first idea that comes to mind. Do you see it? Hear it? Sense or feel it? Know it? Or does the idea appear in several ways simultaneously?

However the idea comes, that is your mind powers at work in the form you typically experience them. Some people are more likely to see visual images; others to hear words; and so on. Whatever way you receive information and ideas is fine. Just be aware of how you do it.

Continue with this exercise a few more times for confirmation and additional insights into yourself. Again close your eyes and wait for the first idea to pop into your mind. Once more notice how the information has come to you. Also ask yourself: Did the idea appear to me in the same way as it did before? Or did I use another way of perceiving it this time?

After you have tried this technique four or five times, you'll have a better sense of how you perceive. For example, you may be consistent in the way you receive information (visually, auditorially, and so forth). Or you may vary extensively, so you readily use different modes of perception. Also, this information can help you decide if you need to develop more abilities in one area (such as the visual, if you tend not to receive any images), or if you want to work towards having more of a balance. For example, if all of your perceptions have been visual or auditory, you may want to increase your ability to trust your intuitive sense of knowing.

2. Measuring Your Intuitive Abilities

To discover how strong your mind power abilities are in each of these four areas—visual, auditory, sensing, and knowing—use your mind powers to tell you. Subsequently, you can call on these powers to track the development of each of your abilities over them.

The way to rate yourself is to close your eyes, get relaxed, and, with a piece of paper and pencil at hand, ask yourself: "How strong are my *visual* abilities on a scale of 0 to 100?" Be aware of the first number that pops into your head and write it down.

Next ask yourself: "How strong are my *auditory* abilities on a scale of 0 to 100?" Again, notice the first number that appears and record it.

Do the same thing for your *sensing or feeling* abilities, and your *knowing* abilities as well.

At the end of this test, you should have an indication of how high you are operating in each area. If you keep track of your results and monitor yourself from time to time, you'll see how you are doing in developing your abilities. You'll find that your inner voice or vision doesn't lie—listen to it, and it will give you an accurate picture of your mind power skills.

SCHEDULING A REGULAR TIME PERIOD FOR PRACTICE

In the beginning, set aside some time for regular practice, just as you would in developing any other skill like writing, typing, or playing tennis. Once you learn the basics and start using these techniques regularly, you can incorporate them into whatever you are doing each day, so you may not need any special practice time. Just realize that as with any other skill, the more consistently you work with these techniques, the more you apply them, the more skilled you become.

To get started, plan on about 20 to 30 minutes a day for practice. Use this time to work on achieving your particular goals, such as feeling less stress at work, improving your typing, or getting the money you need to buy a computer.

You'll find that even when you first start practicing the results will be dramatic. Sometimes you may notice an immediate difference—such as feeling more relaxed when you go to work the next day. Or the change may take a few days, if you are working on acquiring a new skill or earning more money.

Just pay attention to what is happening in your life, and you'll find your small time investment to develop these skills well worth the effort.

CHOOSING A GOOD SETTING TO PRACTICE

Although you can use these techniques anywhere—in fact, you can use them to tune out noises and distractions that bother you—it is best to begin in a quiet place where you can be alone. Or, if some friends or associates want to learn these techniques too, arrange for a place to practice together.

In either case, the place you choose should be free of disruptions, such as doorbells or ringing phones. If either is a possibility, leave a note on the door to request visitors to return as you will be busy for a short time, or turn off your phone (or let the answering machine get it).

It is important to have a quiet place at first, so you can learn to focus and direct your attention. Also, using a regular place to practice helps condition you, so that you're in the appropriate frame of mind to work on these techniques whenever you enter the room. It's much like having an office or studio for certain kinds of work. You know when you're there that it's time to work. So you settle down quickly and do whatever needs to be done.

It also helps to adjust the lighting or use appropriate props, depending on what you want to do. For instance, if you want a soothing, calming effect, or a setting for some deep thinking, low lighting can help create a feeling of calm and quiet. Conversely, if you want to raise your energy for some project (such as writing a report to meet a deadline), strong lighting can help create the mood.

If possible, use some object that reinforces your purpose in doing these exercises. Say you want to close a stock deal. Perhaps place in front of you a newspaper with stock quotes, a stock certificate, or your presentation folder, so you can concentrate on it. If you want a raise, then maybe imagining a pile of money before you might do the trick. You can use anything for a reinforcer. The key is to select a focus that has a relevant meaning for you.

GETTING RELAXED

The key to using any mind power technique is getting relaxed, so you can focus your attention on whatever you want to achieve with that technique. Even if you want to raise your energy to perform some activity, you still have to start in a relaxed state of mind so you can get that one-pointed focus.

Sit in a comfortable position, so you are not only ready to relax but ready to take some action after you attain a relaxed state. Although some people like to lie down to achieve a deeper feeling of relaxation, I prefer the sitting-action mode—and with this approach, you don't have to worry about falling asleep. Close your eyes if you wish.

If you use a sitting position, I recommend sitting straight up on a chair with both feet touching the floor and your hands up or together. This is a comfortable position, and you can use it almost anywhere—in a straight backed office chair, in a soft living room armchair, even on a bus or airplane.

Keep your spine straight and rest your feet on the floor so you feel solidly grounded. At the same time, hold your hands in front of you with the palms up, or place your hands together with your index fingers and thumbs pointing up and touching, so you feel receptive to your feelings and intuitions. If you hold your hands in this special way, they can become a trigger to remind you that you are now tapping into your inner voice. In time, you won't need a special trigger, because you will internalize the process. But in the beginning, these hand positions will help you get in the appropriate mental set to be receptive.

Finally, be sure you are sufficiently warm when you do these exercises. Nothing distracts like feeling chilled.

The following relaxation exercises will help you calm down and get prepared for whatever else you want to do. Work with them at first in your quiet place until you feel comfortable with them. Then, you can do them anywhere—even in a crowd or noisy office; you just have to concentrate harder.

These exercises use three calming approaches:

- focusing on your breath to shift your attention from the distractions and stresses of the outer world to the peaceful inner world
- quieting your body to quiet your mind
- concentrating on a soothing visual image or sound to calm both body and mind

Use whatever approach suits you best, or combine them as you wish.

---

1. FOCUS ON YOUR BREATH   Time: 2-5 minutes

Begin by paying attention to your breathing. Notice your breath going in and out, in and out. Experience the different parts of your body moving up and down, in and out, as you breathe.

With each breath, direct your breath to a different point in your body. Breathe down to your foot, to your hand, and feel your breath flowing in and out.

Now consciously breathe slowly and deeply for ten breaths. As you do, say to yourself: "I am relaxed; I am relaxed."

You should now be relaxed. To get even more so, continue using this, or use another relaxation exercise.

2. QUIET YOUR BODY   Time: 3-5 minutes

Use muscle tension and a feeling of warmth to calm down.

To begin, tighten all your muscles as tight as you can. Clench your fists, your feet, your arms, your legs, your stomach muscles. Clench your teeth; squinch up your face; tense everything. Then release and relax all your muscles as much as you can. Just let everything go, and be aware of the difference. Do this three times.

Now, beginning with your feet and working your way up to your head, concentrate on each body part getting warm and relaxed. As you do, say to yourself: "My (toes, feet, legs, thighs) are now warm and relaxed." Do this sequentially for each body part.

As you do this, you may become aware of certain tensions or tightnesses in certain body areas. If so, you can send healing energy to that part of your body. (See Chapter 13 for a variety of healing techniques).

Continue relaxing each body part in turn. After you have relaxed your head, conclude the exercise by saying to yourself: "Now I am totally calm, totally relaxed, totally ready to experience whatever comes."

3. CONCENTRATE ON A CALMING IMAGE OR SOUND   Time: 2-3 minutes

Use images and sounds to slow yourself down.

There are many calming images and sounds on which you can concentrate. Here are a few possibilities.

- Visualize yourself entering an elevator. Push one of the buttons to descend. As you pass each floor, you become more and more relaxed, more and more relaxed. When you are fully relaxed, step out of the elevator feeling calm and refreshed.
- Visualize yourself by the seashore. Notice the waves and watch them flow in and out, in and out, in and out. As they do, feel yourself becoming calmer and calmer. Then, when you feel fully calm, leave the shore.
- Chant a single syllable or sound like "om" or "ah." As you do this, experience the sound expanding in your head, erasing all other distracting images and thoughts.

KEEPING RECORDS OF WHAT YOU "SEE"

As you use these techniques for insights and ideas, you will find it useful to write this information down or record it on tape. There are several advantages to doing this.

- You won't forget important ideas you get (such as an idea for a valuable invention, cost-cutting procedure, or approach to take in improving relationships with a co-worker).
- You can keep track of your development in achieving a desired goal (such as creating a sales organization), or you can chart your progress in improving your mind power abilities. (For instance, you could keep a weekly rating of your performance percentage in each mind power area.)
- You can record the advice you get for the decisions you make, and later review the results when you follow this advice and when you don't.
- You can write down your insights about what you believe is likely to happen in a given situation. Then assess developments periodically to help you better respond.

I have two books I use for keeping records. One is a *New Ideas Book*, where I jot down ideas I develop with these techniques which have commercial possibilities (such as an idea for a new book, doll, or game).

The other is a *Daily Journal*, where, from time to time, I record significant experiences and insights about what to do next in my life. For example, I usually write down the following: (1) a brief synopsis of any dreams I remember and any reactions or ideas due to this dream; (2) any information I feel is important after a techniques session (such as a monthly goal for activities and earnings), and (3) significant experiences of the day (such as a meeting with someone offering a new business opportunity about which I must make a decision).

You can use any format that works for you. Some people make a regular practice of writing down their ideas and experiences daily; others, like me, only do this to record something that seems especially significant. Use the approach that suits you.

Generally, though, it is useful to keep records in these five major areas:

1. *New ideas you may want to act on.* This is the place to record ideas for new products, new organizational plans, new activities to try, and so forth.
2. *Significant experiences of the day.* This can include things like important meetings or phone calls, intuitions about people or situations, goals or accomplishments you have achieved, predictions or plans for the future, and the like.
3. *Dreams from the night before.* Record as much as you can recall, along with any insights about the dream's meaning. Sometimes, if

you can't remember a dream immediately, meditating for a few minutes right after waking on any dream fragments you recall or on your awareness that you have had a dream may bring the dream back. The value of writing down your dreams is you are more apt to remember them, and you can use your dream insights to help you better understand a current situation and make decisions. For instance, if you are thinking of taking a new job or entering into a business venture with someone and you have a dream showing the person or venture in a negative light, that can be a good sign you shouldn't make the move.

4. *Mind power insights and experiences.* Record any experiences or ideas that stand out after a techniques session. You can record them during the experience (for example, if you are using automatic writing to decide what investments to make), or if it's more convenient, make your record afterwards.

5. *Miscellaneous ideas.* This might be a section at the back of your notebook where you file ideas on mind power methods, statements to think about, illustrations, and so on.

USING MIND POWER TECHNIQUES TO ATTAIN YOUR GOALS

Now you are ready to start using these techniques for specific goals. The rest of this book, accordingly, features exercises you can use to achieve specific objectives, and gives examples of people who have used these techniques successfully.

To use this book most effectively, decide what goal you want to attain, and turn to that section. Then, use the exercises suggested, or, employing the underlying mind power principles, adapt these exercises to make them your own. (For instance, if you'd rather draw a picture of what you see than write a statement about it, do so. If you'd rather get information from a visualization of a library than a computer console, go ahead).

The key to the effectiveness of these exercises is the principle of tapping into your mind power—and you can use any number of images and symbols to do this. The exercises described in this book are ones that have worked for me and others, but feel free to create your own.

 *Chapter 3*

Overcoming Stress and Tension— Learning to Relax

ACHIEVING A BALANCE BETWEEN STRESS, TENSION, AND RELAXATION

Stress is common in the workplace today, and these tensions can carry over into other aspects of life. A key reason for this is the pressure of our competitive, success-oriented age.

There are pressures to perform, to meet deadlines, to do well, to perform better than the competition, to get a contract, to obtain a job, to be promoted, to look successful...and so on. These pressures are too well known to need much explanation. They come with the territory of trying to accomplish and succeed.

A little stress can be stimulating and encourage people to do even better. For example, when a speaker feels a twinge of anxiety before giving a talk, he or she usually does very well, because that small amount of stress triggers extra adrenalin, so the speaker has more energy and is primed for performing. But when the stress level gets too high, it interferes with performance—and may even make performance impossible. Instead of pushing the person to peak performance, the extra energy becomes unmanageable and turns into a serious case of nerves. A good performance, even any performance, may be blocked.

By the same token, when a person worries a little about meeting a deadline, that can stimulate him or her to get on the stick and 15 accomplish what needs to be done. But with too many worries, a person can get caught up in a vicious cycle in which these negative thoughts become the focus of attention and shut out the creative, productive thoughts that contribute to accomplishing the goal.

Thus, learning to relax and getting rid of unwanted tension becomes critical for working effectively in the workplace and having a satisfying, successful life. The key is to watch for signs that one is overtense or overstressed, and then work on creating an appropriate balance between the slight tension needed to stimulate effective performance and the need to be sufficiently relaxed to feel confident, composed, and carry out any task smoothly and efficiently.

Select the relaxation or stress reduction techniques that feel most comfortable for you.

HOW MIND POWER TECHNIQUES CAN HELP

The following case histories illustrate some examples of how well mind power techniques can help you relax and get rid of unwanted stress.

Dave G., was a typical type-A executive. He was head of the marketing and sales department for a small manufacturing company in communications, and was always rushing around from one appointment to another, determined to put everything he had into closing the deal. He drove the handful of sales people under him the same way, and when anyone didn't make a sale, he carefully grilled the person about what went wrong. Likewise, when he failed to make a sale himself or didn't sell as much as he thought he could, he mentally castigated himself for "screwing up."

Not surprisingly, he experienced a high level of turnover in his sales organization, and he often felt like a bundle of nerves himself when he went out on a sales call. In fact, his doctor had warned him he would be a good candidate for an ulcer if he kept going on this way.

Instead, Dave needed to learn how to relax and let go of the day-to-day pressures he felt, which grew out of his strong fear of failure. His first step in letting go was becoming aware of when he felt particularly anxious, and reminding himself that he needed to release that tension.

When this happened, he tried to conclude whatever he was doing as quickly as possible, and spend some time in his office alone. Or, if he was on the road, Dave would park his car in a quiet spot, turn off the radio, and concentrate on quieting his mind.

Then, using one of the calming exercises described in Chapter 2, he focused on calming down. He took a few minutes to pay attention to his breathing, tightened and released his muscles, or saw himself getting more relaxed as he went down from floor to floor in an elevator.

After a few minutes, these relaxation exercises took effect, and he felt his tension dissipate. However, to prevent the anxiety from returning once he went back to work, he asked his inner mind what he needed to do to stay relaxed. He remained in his relaxed, meditative state of mind to ask this and framed the question mentally: "Why am I so tense right now?" Then he asked "What do I need to do to stay calm?"

After he asked each question, he listened for the answer. The response to the first question came quickly: "You must let go of your need to have to make the sale. You must listen to the customer and then do your best. But do not blame yourself or your salespeople for not succeeding. Just do your best and tell them to do the same. You can't expect to achieve 100 percent all the time."

In answer to his second question, the voice said: "Keep reminding yourself what you must do. Tell yourself you must let go and stop blaming yourself. Tell yourself you must do your best, and that's all you can expect. When you feel tense, tell yourself: 'I am relaxed. I am letting go. I am doing the best I can. I am relaxed.' And keep saying this to yourself for as long as you need to. Then, you'll calm down and be fine."

Once he got these answers, Dave returned to work, repeating these messages to himself and determined to let go, listen, and do his best, without feeling he *had* to succeed. At first, he had a bit of a struggle to keep away the usual thoughts about accomplishment that contributed to his anxieties. But gradually, as he repeated these exercises, he found the periods of relaxation and reduced tension lasted longer and longer, until finally even the people around him noticed the change.

His salespeople found his disposition sunnier and they felt motivated to work harder. Also, they performed better as he eased his demands on them. At the same time, he found his own negotiations improved, for he was less intense and driving with his customers, so they could feel more relaxed working with him. In turn, as he listened to them more and learned more about what they wanted, he was better able to create win-win solutions that led to additional sales and a higher average volume for each one. Then, as his own sales and the sales of others in his department went up, Dave felt more confident and relaxed. In time, he no longer needed to use these exercises; the problem was over. However, the mind power techniques had triggered the initial relaxation and tension reduction that led to his ultimate success.

Similarly, Melinda used these techniques to get rid of the feelings of pressure she felt as a freelance researcher with a part-time business selling specialty foods. In her late 30s, she had once gone through an anti-establishment period, when she felt time commitments and agreements didn't matter. The emphasis then was on "doing your own thing when you wanted," and she felt totally relaxed and tension-free.

However, as the interest of her friends and associates shifted to business concerns and making a living, she realized that she needed to run her life differently, and after taking a series of workshops on prosperity, dressing for success, setting goals, and time management, she reoriented her life around being successful in business. In this spirit, she began making lists of goals, prioritizing everything she did, and setting schedules that she was determined to meet.

The only problem was that her efforts to accomplish these objectives made her feel very tense. She began to worry that she couldn't accomplish her objectives, and she pushed herself to perform as quickly as she could to finish a project. In turn, due to these rigid requirements, she felt very rushed and pressured and often felt her stomach churning or in knots. At the same time, she experienced no joy in doing the project and no satisfaction when she completed it—only a relieved feeling that the work was done and now there was one less thing to do. Meanwhile, her side business felt like one more pressure on her, and instead of enjoying the meetings with others in the business, she felt drained and overextended.

Eventually, though, like Dave, she was able to turn a stressful situation around by using the power of her mind to find the answers she needed so she could learn to relax. She began with the usual relaxation techniques to calm down and get in a meditative frame of mind. Then she asked her inner mind the two questions: "Why am I so tense right now?" and "What do I need to do to stay calm?"

Her first answer was something she might have easily known but hadn't thought about before: "You have placed too many requirements on yourself. You must not ask so much of yourself. You must learn to be more flexible. You don't need to try to do everything. You shouldn't expect to be Superwoman."

Then, when she asked what to do to stay calm, her answer sounded like common sense—as is often the message of one's intuition. But because she had been so caught up in creating and keeping her schedules, she had never slowed up enough to think about what to do. Her inner voice told her she should: "Continue to set goals and work out schedules, but be willing to change them. Only do what is most important first, and try to accomplish it as best you can as soon as possible. If you can't do it right away, reschedule some time to accomplish it later. And tell yourself each day: I'm relaxed. I'm flexible. I'm doing the best I can. If I accomplish my goal immediately, great. If not, I must learn to wait and be patient. All things will come in due course. I just need to do my best."

The results for Melinda were much like those experienced by Dave. Gradually, she learned to place less pressure on herself, and increasingly, she felt more relaxed and less tense. In turn, with the pressure off, she was able to accomplish more and do it more effectively, and her confidence increased about what she could do.

THE STEPS TO OVERCOMING STRESS AND TENSION

The examples just described illustrate the basic steps to reducing and eliminating unwanted stress and tension. These are:

1. Calm Down with a Relaxation Technique.

You can use any of the techniques described in Chapter 2 for this. In addition, develop a trigger for yourself, so whenever you feel sensations of stress coming on, you can catch yourself and remain calm and relaxed. To create this trigger, end your relaxation exercise with a suggestion that whenever you want to relax, you will do one of the following:

- bring together the thumb and middle forefinger of your right hand;
- say to yourself several times: "I am calm. I am relaxed."; or
- create your own triggering device that suggests relaxation to you.

Then, during the day, whenever you feel under pressure, use your trigger to help yourself calm down. For instance, suppose you have an important strategy meeting with your boss or co-workers coming up and you feel nervous about it. Just before the meeting is a good time to use your trigger to tell yourself you feel calm and relaxed. Or you might do even more, as will be discussed in other chapters, to tell yourself you feel confident; or perhaps mentally picture the meeting going exactly as you want, so you are more likely to get the outcome you want.

The advantage of this relaxation approach is it helps calm you down and relieves mild symptoms of stress. However, it doesn't deal with the underlying reasons you are feeling stressed. So for a deeper, more permanent solution, you need to take additional steps to understand what you are doing to make yourself tense, and learn how you can get rid of this source of tension by coming up with alternative actions.

2. Understand the Sources of Your Stress or Tension

To find out the reason you feel tense, get in a relaxed frame of mind and mentally ask yourself the question, as did Dave and Melinda: "Why am I so tense right now?" Then, listen to whatever thoughts immediately pop into mind or notice any images that appear. You will find that encouraging this spontaneity will give you insights into your inner feelings and concerns.

If you have any difficulty getting a full response to your question, you can do two things to spur your inner processes.

- You can imagine that you are talking to an inner guide or counselor, or that you are getting the information you seek on a computer console or movie screen.

- You can write down any thoughts or images on a sheet of paper using an automatic writing process to make your thoughts flow more freely.

3. Decide What You Need to Do to Get Rid of This Source of Tension

Once you have determined the reason for your stress in a particular situation, the next step is asking yourself what you should do about it. Again, if you trust your mind powers, you will find your inner self has the answers about what to do.

Thus, it's now time to ask the second question Dave and Melinda used: "What do I need to do to stay calm?" Again, don't try to shape your answer consciously, but be receptive to what your inner mind tells you. Then, to get more information, ask a further question: "What else must I do to stay calm?"

As before, the key to communicating with your inner powers is encouraging your inner spontaneity to tell you the information you need to know. Once again, use an inner guide, counselor, screen, or automatic writing to encourage the process if you encounter any resistance to your question.

4. Chase Away Any Worries About the Problem

The final step is to chase away any worries and fears about achieving the results you want. These worries are like an internal negative dialogue we have with ourselves in which we state all the can'ts preventing us from doing something, or we assert our fears about why what we want won't occur. But such concerns are totally unproductive and do nothing but increase our feelings of stress.

For instance, take that important strategy meeting described earlier. You may already feel anxious and tense, as you consider it very important to make a good impression. But worries take away your inner confidence that you can do it. Instead, they get you concerned that maybe you can't, that you won't be good enough, that the other people in the meeting may not understand, and so forth.

In short, your worries lead you to churn the situation over and over in your mind, because you're afraid how the event will turn out and you fear the worst. The result is your worries make you feel terrible, and your negative thoughts contribute to the very outcome you fear. For instance, if you're worried you won't give a good presentation, you probably won't. You'll lack the confidence you need, and your whole manner will convey the impression: "I don't think I'm any good." Furthermore, your worries can interfere with implementing the answers you get about methods to relieve stress, as they can lead you to think these techniques won't work.

Thus, if you've got any worries or fears standing in the way of overcoming your feelings of tension, you've got to eliminate them, and you can do so in four ways:

- Come up with an alternative, so you can act to affect the situation.
- Visualize the outcome you want, and your focus on this will help bring about the desired result.
- Remind yourself that you will do it to build confidence.
- Affirm that whatever happens is what should happen, so you can accept what comes and feel satisfied with it.

Depending on the situation, use any one or a combination of these techniques. Then, when you are done, turn your thoughts to something else, unless you have planned to take a specific action, so the inner powers released by your concentration can work within you to help create the change you want.

---

1. COME UP WITH AN ALTERNATIVE   Time: 3-5 minutes

See yourself as the director of a movie. You are sitting in your director's chair on a film set, which is in the same location as where you are having your current problem. You also have a script in your hands which is about this problem. The actors are waiting in the wings for their cue to start playing out this script, and one of the characters represents you.

Now, as you watch for a few moments, the characters act out the events leading up to the present situation. For example, if this is a work problem, the actors will be your boss, work associates, or employees. If you are worried about a business deal, you will see yourself in negotiations with the principal players. The characters play the scene just as you have remembered it.

As the action comes to the present time, go over to the director and ask: "What does the script say I should do now?" Then listen to the reply. The director may have several suggestions that you can try. Or he may tell you to wait and relax. If the director is uncertain, this tells you that you should do nothing actively now to affect the situation (although you can visualize the outcome you want or affirm your willingness to accept whatever comes.)

Whatever the results, feel you can trust this inner voice, so there is no need to worry any longer. Then, act, wait, or relax as suggested, and feel confident that the appropriate outcome will occur.

2. VISUALIZE THE DESIRED OUTCOME   Time: 3-5 minutes

If you already know the outcome you would like, visualize that occurring to make those results more likely. For example, if you want your co-workers to go along with your suggestions at a meeting, see yourself presenting a forceful argument and see them agreeing with what you have to say. Meanwhile, as you see this outcome, feel confident it will happen, so you can put any worries about the results out of your mind.

To reinforce your visualization, use the following telegram technique:

See yourself in a private office at work. Even if you don't currently have a private office, imagine that you do, and it is very comfortable and quiet. Now, imagine it is the present and you are thinking about the situation that has been bothering you.

Suddenly, there is a knock on the door. You get up, answer it, and a messenger hands you a telegram, which says on it in big red letters: "Urgent and important."

You open the telegram, read it, and feel ecstatic, because the telegram informs you that everything is the way you would like it to be. For example, if you are concerned about a presentation, you are giving a good one. If you are worried about a promotion, you are getting it. If you are having problems with a co-worker, all is resolved.

Now, for the next few minutes, concentrate on seeing the desired situation before you. You have exactly what you want.

3. REMIND YOURSELF YOU WILL DO IT   Time: 1 minute

You can also chase away your fears about something you have to do by building up your confidence that you can do it. A simple way to do this is to remind yourself from time to time during the day that you can and will do it.

Take a few quiet minutes now and then to get calm and centered and say to yourself several times, with intense concentration:

"I can do it (fill in the image of whatever you want to do). I am doing it (fill in the image of yourself doing it)."

The key is to see yourself doing whatever you wish to do in the here and now, so your inner mind gets used to your doing it. Also, feel a sense of assurance and confidence that you are doing this activity correctly and effectively. Perhaps visualize others being pleased and complimenting you on whatever you have done (such as writing a good report, giving a good presentation, leading a successful meeting).

You'll feel better immediately. You'll be calmer, more relaxed, less worried about whatever you have to do. In addition, when it comes time to perform the activity, you'll do it better, because you feel more confident and you have already rehearsed it in your mind.

4. AFFIRM YOUR ACCEPTANCE   Time 3-5 minutes

Sometimes, no matter how much you try to actively or mentally influence events, circumstances may not turn out as you hoped. You don't get a desired transfer or promotion; you suddenly find an expected client doesn't come through. Yet, often, in the long run, things will turn out for the best, if you are only patient. For example, Jane D. felt very depressed for several days when she didn't get a research project assignment, after she wrote up a twenty-page proposal for the project. But a few weeks later, she learned about an even bigger project, and using the information she had put together for her original proposal, she was able to turn out an excellent response to the project administrators in record time. They were impressed, and she got the job.

Thus, one important key to overcoming worries is to realize that often things may seem to go wrong, but we can turn them around or use what goes wrong as a learning experience to create something even better. Still another way to think of initially undesirable events is to realize that often our wants and needs differ, and when they do, we usually get what we need. For example, a person longs for a new job title with additional responsibilities and a new office. But, in fact, the person hasn't had sufficient experience to handle the job, and would find himself over his head and perhaps fired if he were promoted right away.

Thus, it is important to develop a feeling of acceptance about whatever happens, as well as trying to do your best to achieve your goals. In other words, if you truly feel you have done everything possible to attain a goal but don't get it, be accepting of this outcome. The important thing is you have done your all, and now it's time to be receptive and patient until the next opportunity presents itself.

The value of this approach is that you are aligning yourself with the flow of events, rather than fighting against the current. Further, you are basing your actions on the premise that nothing in the universe happens by coincidence, but rather the universe seems to respond to our needs by providing exactly what we require. Thus, what happens is what should.

In turn, if you use this premise to guide your life, you will find everything much easier for you. You'll still try as hard as you can to attain your goals. Yet you'll also feel a sense of satisfaction and completion regardless of what happens, knowing that somehow you can profit from the experience and consider it to be for the best in the long run.

The following visualization will help you develop this power of acceptance.

See yourself seated in a park near where you work. The sun is shining brightly, and it is very quiet and peaceful. You are enjoying a lunch break, and you feel very calm, relaxed, and receptive to whatever comes.

Now, from the distance, some people arrive carrying small wrapped packages tied with ribbons. These people look like they might have come from one of the stores in your neighborhood, and they come over to you and hand you the packages as a gift.

As you open each package you find a different present inside. It may be some money, an object, a certificate providing some service to you. Some gifts you want; others you need; others are unexpected. But as you open each gift, you receive it with the same spirit of equal acceptance, and you say simply to the person who gave it to you: "Thank you, I accept." Then, that person turns and goes, and you receive and open the next package.

You continue receiving these gifts, until all of the gift bearers have finished giving them to you and leave.

Remind yourself that these gifts represent the experiences and challenges you encounter in life. And just like you have received and accepted each gift, you must receive and accept each experience that comes like a gift. You must participate to the best of your ability, and use the experience to learn from and grow. But whatever it is, you must learn to accept it.

For this is the secret of staying calm and relaxed, overcoming stress, and getting rid of worries. You must learn to receive and accept, as well as try to achieve and grow.

 *Chapter 4*

Increase Your Energy and Overcome Fatigue

John P. used to feel totally exhausted every few months when he had to meet major deadlines as a freelance writer and designer. Suddenly, everyone had a project to be done right away, and he hated to turn any client down, because business was so unpredictable. He never knew when this flurry of activity would end and he would go into a slow period. Thus, he tried to take on everything, but the penalty was that he often felt draggy and knocked out. However, once be began using his mind power abilities to increase his energy, he was able to revive himself, so he could keep going and get everything done.

Similarly, there were times Maggie F., a secretary in a large office, had dozens of things to do and didn't feel like doing them. She had been to a big party the night before; she was thinking about an upcoming dinner date; she had a wonderful weekend planned and thoughts about it kept intruding; she wasn't inspired by the particular project she was assigned; or she felt a little miffed at a slight by her boss. Still, she knew she had to get her mind behind her work and motivate herself to do it. At one time, she might have tried a few cups of coffee, perhaps a pep pill to get herself going again. But instead, by mobilizing the powers of her mind, she could give herself the energy charge she needed to get to work, without using anything artificial.

We all have times like these. However, like John and Maggie, you need a quick energy fix to overcome feelings of fatigue, increase your creative energy, and motivate yourself to do something. These mind power techniques are ideal in the following types of situations.

- You feel draggy or sleepy during the day.
- You have to start a big project and feel overwhelmed by all you have to do, so you resist getting started.
- You don't feel motivated to work on a project, although you know you have to do it.
- You have to come up with some ideas for a project and feel your creative energy is blocked.
- You have to be alert and enthusiastic for some activity, such as making a sales call, giving a speech, or leading a meeting.
- You need something to get you going in the morning and keep you going at night.

WORKING THE MIND POWER TECHNIQUES

In all of these situations and in others where you need a quick charge of energy to get moving again, these mind power techniques work because you are using your imagination and thoughts to create the energy you need. As a result, you don't need to use anything artificial like pep pills, which can upset your body chemistry and have unpleasant side effects. Instead, you are drawing the energy you need from inside you, from the energy of the earth and air around you, or from a combination of these sources—whatever feels best for you. You do this by imagining that you have columns of energy flowing into and through you. You can imagine the energy of the earth as more solid and grounding, the energy of the air or cosmos as more light and expansive, and your own energy as a mingling of the two. Use these images to draw on the energy you feel you need most.

You can obtain energy from these sources, as everything in the universe is made up of molecules of energy. These molecules come together to form material objects, including you, and your thoughts are waves of energy, too. At the lower theta, delta, and alpha frequencies, associated with sleep and meditation, our thoughts are moving more slowly, while at the beta frequency associated with everyday thinking, we are more active and alert. In turn, the frequencies of our thoughts can influence the frequencies of our bodies.

Thus, when you use your mind powers to concentrate on raising your energy level, you are actually stimulating the molecules of energy in your body to move more quickly, so you not only feel more energetic but become more energetic. By the same token, when you focus on drawing in energy from the universe, the imagery of this energy serves to activate your body.

The following techniques will rouse you to whatever you have to do. The first technique: *Creating Your Own Energy and Enthusiasm* is particularly good for a situation in which you need a quick rush of energy to wake up, keep going, or feel more enthusiastic and motivated. The second technique, *Drawing on the Energies of the Universe,* is ideal if you have to generate the energy or creative spark to work on a big project.

---

1. CREATING YOUR OWN ENERGY AND ENTHUSIASM   Time: About 1 minute

Stand with your feet slightly apart and make a fist with one hand. Then, quickly raise your hand to your head and lower it several times. Each time you bring it down, shout out something like: "I am awake," "I feel energetic," "I am enthusiastic and excited," or "I am raring to get up and go." Do this five to ten times.

As you do this, feel a rush of energy and enthusiasm surge through you, and soon you'll be awake and alert and ready to tackle any project.

If other people are around so you can't actively participate in this exercise, imagine yourself doing it in your mind's eye. It's more stimulating to use your whole body, but using your mind powers alone will help wake you up or motivate you to act.

2. DRAWING ON THE ENERGIES OF THE UNIVERSE   Time: 2-3 minutes

In this technique, you imagine the energies of the earth and the cosmos coursing through you to give you the energy you need to do something you want to do.

Begin by sitting with your spine straight, your feet on the floor, your hands up to receive the energy, and your eyes closed.

Now see the energy of the earth coming up through the ground and surging into your body. Feel it rising through your feet, through your legs, to the base of your spine, and expanding out through your torso, into your arms and head. Feel its strength into your arms and head. Feel its strength and its power.

Meanwhile, as the earth energy surges through you, see the energy of the universe coming in through the top of your head, into your spine, into your arms, and spiraling down through your torso. Notice that this energy feels light, airy, expansive.

Then, focus on the two energies meeting at the base of your spine, and see them join and spiral around together—moving up and down your spine and filling you with energy. You can balance the two energies, if you wish, by drawing on extra energy from the earth (heavy) or from the universe (light) as you wish.

Keep running this energy up and down your spine until you feel filled with energy.

Now, if you have a project or task you want to do, direct this energy towards doing this project. If you haven't felt motivated to do it, notice that you feel motivated and excited to begin work on this project now. If you have been resisting doing something because there is so much to do, be aware that you now have the energy and enthusiasm to tackle the project, and you feel confident you can do it. If you have felt your creativity blocked, experience your creative juices flowing now, and know that you are able to perform this task.

As you direct this energy, see it flowing out of you as needed so you can do this project. For example, if you want to write or type something, visualize the energy surging out through your hands. If you plan to lift some heavy objects, visualize the energy coming out through your feet, body, and hands. Whatever you need to do, see the energy coursing through you as needed, so you can do whatever you want to do.

After you finish this exercise, plunge immediately into your project. You'll suddenly have lots of energy and enthusiasm.

HOW I ENERGIZE MYSELF WITH MIND POWER

I have found these techniques invaluable in my own work. For example, when I first started writing regularly for clients, I used the *Energies of the Universe* technique for the first few weeks to start my day, so I felt ready and motivated to write. I knew I had to meet certain deadlines, and I didn't want to leave anything to chance.

Thus, each morning I began by sitting in my living room and visualizing the energy pouring into me and swirling around through me. Then I pictured it pouring out of me into the writing assignment I had for that day. As a result, I went to the typewriter feeling confident I could do whatever was required, and I felt enthusiastic and motivated to get to work right away. After a few weeks I had conditioned myself to begin working every time I went to the typewriter, so I no longer needed to continue doing the exercises for this purpose. But initially, this technique proved invaluable in getting me on a regular writing schedule, so I could complete my assignments successfully.

In other situations, where I have not yet conditioned myself, I still use this exercise. For instance, sometimes when I have to give a class or seminar and don't feel in the mood, I'll use this technique to feel up and inspired. I'll imagine the energy pouring through me, and in this case, coming out through my voice. Similarly, if I have a lot of telephone calls to make and find the task a little awesome, I'll use this technique for the energy I need to pick up the phone and make each call with enthusiasm.

Frequently, too, I'll use the first energy technique as a quick pick-me-up during the day. For instance, I've used it at seminars and conferences to wake myself up when I felt I was drifting off. I'd simply concentrate on being awake and alert in my mind's eye, and repeat a key phrase (such as "I'm enthusiastic and excited" or "I'm alert and awake.") again and again in my mind. Then, in a few minutes, I typically feel ready to go or listen again.

This technique isn't designed to be a replacement for the sleep you need. If you keep drifting off while doing something and find you're continually tired afterwards, you obviously need some more sleep. But on a short-term basis, this technique is ideal for a quick energy fix.

 *Chapter 5*

Increasing Your Confidence and Feelings of Self-Esteem for Greater Success

Being confident is one of the keys to getting what you want in life. In turn, as you get what you want, you feel more confident and have more self-esteem.

It's a reciprocal process that starts with building confidence, although often, when people are just starting out in something, they don't feel confident, which can create problems. For when you don't have confidence in yourself, it's easy for others to break you down with the slightest criticism about you or what you're doing. Then, without a firm sense of self, you can easily start agreeing with them and tear yourself down, rather than viewing any criticism objectively as an opinion about your behavior rather than a critique of yourself. The advantage of seeing things objectively is you can turn any criticism into a chance to change and grow if you feel the criticism is a good one; or disregard it as an observation you don't agree with if you feel the criticism is wrong.

33

I learned this principle myself when I was first starting my business about fifteen years ago. I began with plenty of doubts. I had developed some game ideas that people seemed to like, was bored with my market research job at an ad agency and felt underpaid for what I was doing (this was back when men were paid much more than women for the same job). I got some financial help from my mother and decided to try it on my own.

But in those days, it was very easy to shake my confidence. I didn't know anything about mind power techniques, and I was readily swayed by anyone's opinion about anything, no matter how wrong. For example, I listened when an artist suggested using a dramatic photograph of the game pieces in a party game on the cover, rather than a drawing of people playing the game and having fun. Also I listened when people said I should have all sorts of promotional materials, like flags, posters, and buttons, which only ended up costing money—lots of it—and did nothing for sales.

At the same time, I was very unsure of the value of my ideas. I remember driving to Los Angeles with an educator who was going to show some games, including several of mine, to a game company, and feeling very nervous about the whole process. The educator said my ideas were good, but I wasn't sure, and I needed the confirmation of the game company to feel my work had any value. Also, I felt the correctness of my decision to leave the security of an advertising job was on the line, and I was continually worrying if I had done the right thing. I don't know what I would have done if the game company had rejected my idea at this crucial time. Probably, I would have taken it as a rejection of me as well as my idea, and that might have changed the course of my life, because I didn't have that sense of inner knowing, the inner mind power, to back me up regardless of what anyone else said.

As it happened, the company did decide to publish my game, and that gave me the confidence I needed to continue along my freelance path. Yet, even so, I continually needed outside feedback with each new project to give me the confidence I didn't have within. Gradually, as I published more games, I felt a little more sure of what I was doing. But still, that inner self-assurance, so necessary to real success, was lacking.

The problem with having this lack is that a person who is negative, critical, and judgmental can easily tear you down, and if you are around this person long enough, he or she can potentially destroy you. For example, if you have a boss or co-worker like this and you don't feel secure in yourself, it can be devastating to your morale. You start taking this person's assessment of you as your own, and you start tearing yourself down. You think: "He or she thinks I'm wrong, so I must be," and pretty soon you conclude: "I am wrong." And when that happens, your confidence and self-image are destroyed.

For example, I experienced this problem before I began my rebuilding process and started discovering and developing the mind power techniques described in this book. I had built up a fairly good track record in getting games on the market—nearly twenty at this point, when an artist I'll call Richard approached me. He had an idea for a line of poster games to be played on a wall, and he wanted me to create the games and write the copy, while he did the art work. My initial thought was: "Who wants to stand at a wall to play a game, and maybe we should do a market test first to see if anyone is interested in buying this." But Richard seemed confident, and, besides, he had found a company that was willing to put money into the idea. So I pushed my initial reservations aside after briefly mentioning them. Richard poohpoohed these concerns saying a market test would be an unnecessary and time-consuming expense and I meekly went along with his assessment. Today, knowing what I do about trusting one's inner feelings, I wouldn't do this. But at the time, I was so eager for approval from someone else to give me confidence that I agreed to just about anything.

I also ignored other warning signs I would never overlook today. A key danger signal, for instance, was that I didn't feel good about working with this artist. He was negative, snappy, had a waspish personality, and, as the project went on, I found he had a tendency to blame anything that went wrong on others—commonly on his wife (now his ex) and on me. When this happened, there was no way to discuss the problem rationally. He would fly into a tantrum and rage and yell. Today, I would walk out on this situation very early—or more probably, I would trust my initial reaction, and not work with this person at all. But then, I meekly accepted the situation, and didn't attempt to fight back or leave. So after a while, my confidence sunk even lower, and as Richard's behavior became increasingly critical—sometimes outrageously so (for instance, he even began criticizing the perfectly normal way I said hello when I answered the phone)—I increasingly began to blame myself because I gradually came to see myself through his eyes.

In the end, the entire project collapsed in the marketplace as I suspected it would in the beginning. Consumers didn't buy the posters, as they were not interested in playing tic tac toe, chess, or checkers on a wall, and the posters with new games did even worse. Eventually, I fled to Europe for the summer to get away from both the project and Richard.

When I returned, I felt like I never wanted to invent another game, and I went back to school to get my Ph.D. in sociology, which eventually led to my discovering the powers of the mind. This happened when I began to study spiritual growth groups and realized that their practices were based on an underlying premise that the mind creates the reality the person experiences.

To be sure, my encounter with Richard may seem like an extreme case. But the point is that when you don't have an inner feeling of personal esteem, you are fair game for other people's perceptions of you, and you can easily get sucked into letting that vision put you down. In turn, that can translate into many negatives such as not asking for and therefore not getting what you want at work. Then, too, if you don't feel confident about what you are worth, you will evaluate yourself less favorably and will get less too—less money, less benefits, less prestige, less power, less of everything in all areas of life.

By contrast, when you put your mind power abilities to work to build up your confidence and self-esteem, you will not only feel better, but you'll get much more of everything you want. You will ask for it, you will feel you deserve it, and other people will agree, too. Your attitude will convey that message, and as other people get your message, they can't help but agree.

HOW TO CHANGE YOUR SELF-IMAGE TO CHANGE YOUR LIFE

I know many people who were able to turn their lives around and become successful in their chosen careers by starting with a change in attitude. They started off feeling unsure of themselves, and ended up feeling confident by focusing on their good qualities, seeing themselves as successful, and visualizing themselves being prosperous and recognized by others for their efforts and achievements.

The reason this approach works is because *if you believe you are great, you are great!* And you need to start out with that belief first, because that belief helps to create the experiences you have that support this belief. For example, if you are convinced you should have a certain job or promotion, you'll exude an aura of confidence and act like you belong in that job, so people will think of you in that role. Also, with that belief, you'll know you can do whatever is required and will be able to do it. And soon, you'll find you have that job as you create the reality to reflect your belief.

Certainly external circumstances and the luck of being in the right place at the right time can help you gain confidence. For example, I gained more confidence when I was starting out in the game business as people told me they liked my ideas. But if you lack that inner self-assurance, all the luck and favorable circumstances won't give you that feeling of personal power you need to keep things going well for you.

As an example, think of the many people who get promoted to a new position at work, and then, for various reasons, find they can't handle the additional responsibilities. In effect, it's the Peter Principle in operation—the principle that people get promoted until they reach their level of incompetence. However, underlying the operations of this principle are the old attitudes some people bring to a new position. Whether consciously or unconsciously, they still see themselves in their old roles, and they don't truly feel confident to expand their levels of performance. They feel they don't deserve promotions, are unworthy, and the like. As a result, they eventually screw up so they can drop back down to where they feel comfortable.

By contrast, when you feel that inner confidence, you have that "I can do it whatever it is" feeling, and you're ready to take on new tasks and responsibilities and grow. Because you believe you can do it, you can.

Thus, it all comes back to belief. *You must believe you have the power to create the success you want, and then that belief will give you the power you need to do this*, as the following cases show.

How Joan S. Put Her Dreams in Motion

For example, Joan S. worked at a series of secretarial and paralegal jobs, although she felt stifled. She had many creative ideas and a strong desire for freedom; but she was afraid to make a move. What she really wanted to do was set up her own fashion design business. But she kept thinking about all the barriers that stood in the way—such as not having much money, not having experience, and not having the equipment or employees to get started. Underlying all her thoughts about barriers, was her fear that she didn't have the ability to do what she wanted.

Thus, for several years she continued to work as a secretary and paralegal, although she felt unfulfilled and the desire to break away kept gnawing at her. Then, one weekend she took a workshop where she learned how to imagine what she wanted and affirm that she could get it. In her imagination, there were no barriers, no "I can'ts", no reasons why she couldn't achieve all she desired. Instead, everything she wanted was right there, and she merely had to think out the steps she needed to take to begin the process (such as contacting some outlets to distribute her work, making a few designs after work until she had enough clients to quit, and developing a portfolio of photographs so others could begin showing her work to sell it).

The workshop gave her the initial feeling of assurance that she could do it if she committed herself to her goal, and as a result, she stopped dwelling on the barriers she had created to prevent herself from trying and failing. Instead, she began creatively thinking of what she needed to do right now on a limited budget to get the process into motion. As a result, she started immediately working towards her dream, convinced she would ultimately get it.

Joan S. is still working towards that goal and has a long way to go until it is completely attained. But she is spending about half her days now creating designs and making her goal happen, while doing her secretarial/paralegal work part time. She also feels confident about her own abilities, and, increasingly, she is getting reinforcement for that belief from those who are buying her designs. She also feels fulfilled that she is now doing what she wants. In turn, what she is doing now started with her initial belief in herself. It took those feelings of self-worth and self-esteem to motivate her to work toward her goal.

How Frank S. Changed His Attitude—and Changed His Life

Similarly, Frank F. changed his attitude about himself to get a raise. He worked in the bookkeeping department of a small management consulting company, and he felt he had been passed over unfairly in the company's last two semiannual employee salary reviews. He believed he deserved a raise, and he was particularly resentful because other employees who had been with the company for less time than himself had gotten raises. A few had received more impressive job titles at the same time.

For several months, Frank suffered in silence, and then he went to a class incorporating mind power techniques. He began thinking about all of his good qualities and how his skills were important to his employers. He also considered what he must do to make his employers value his skills more highly, and he realized that they placed a strong emphasis on how their management people looked at work. Thus, he realized he needed to upgrade his image by getting some clothes that looked a little sharper. Additionally, he imagined himself confidently asking his boss for a raise by explaining why his boss should raise his salary.

Frank practiced these techniques for about a week, and as he did, he felt more and more confident about what he expected to do. He began to realize he was worth the additional raise, rather than feeling resentful that others got raises when he didn't. Also, he invested in a new slim-line suit and maroon tie that gave him a more authoritative look.

Then, with his new assurance, based on recognizing his greater self-worth, Frank approached his boss. He began talking about his worth to the company; how he had shown his commitment and loyalty over the years; how be believed in working out win-win situations; and how he hoped his boss would understand the fairness of what he was going to suggest. Finally, he proposed the raise.

The result of this careful preparation was that Frank not only got his raise, but he gained a promotion, too, within a few days. His boss suddenly saw Frank in a new light and was impressed. He realized that Frank could do more than he was doing and gave him new responsibilities to match.

Again, the change in Frank's life had come about as a result of an attitude shift first. Frank had looked within himself to develop more confidence and feelings of self-worth. Then those feelings had translated into change in the everyday world.

HOW TO BUILD UP YOUR CONFIDENCE AND SELF-ESTEEM

The key to building up your confidence and self-esteem and overcoming fears, anxieties, self-doubts, and limiting beliefs, such as "I can't do it" or "I'm not good enough," is to focus on what you can do, know you can do it, and see yourself doing it. Then, using these mind power techniques, you can reverse those fears and anxieties and gain the confidence you need to meet the challenges you face successfully and feel good again. In fact, you can use these techniques to prevent any fears about yourself from creeping into your life by using these methods on a regular basis to affirm that you have the ability to do whatever you want. Further, you can use these techniques to feel confident, because you are fully in charge of the situation.

These are five key ways to build your esteem with these techniques.

1. Become aware of and acknowledge your good qualities, talents, and accomplishments.

2. Affirm that you have the qualities you want to develop, and keep affirming this as you work on developing these qualities.

3. Visualize yourself as a successful person achieving some goal or being recognized for your efforts.

4. See yourself as a prosperous, abundant person, with everything you want.

5. Feel confident, self-assured, and in charge wherever you are.

---

1. RECOGNIZE YOUR GOOD QUALITIES, TALENTS, AND ACCOMPLISHMENTS   Time: About 5 minutes

Whenever we think about what we do well, it's a form of self-affirmation that builds confidence and makes us feel good. But sometimes we forget about our good qualities and talents or don't give ourselves sufficient credit for how much we have already accomplished, particularly when we encounter difficulties and challenges in life—such as a difficult project to complete by a deadline we're not sure we can meet.

To counteract such anxieties about ourselves, we need to remind ourselves what we have and what we can do. This shores up our self-image and helps us feel more sure of ourselves again, because we think: I did it in the past. I have the ability to do it. So I can do it now!

The following technique is a good way to start thinking positively about yourself.

Get a sheet of paper and a pencil, divide the paper into three columns, and head each one: "My Good Qualities," "What I Can Do Well," and "What I Have Accomplished."

Then, close your eyes and meditate on each heading for about a minute or two. What pops into your mind? Don't analyze or question what comes. Just pay attention. After you feel finished, open your eyes, and write down your good qualities, talents, or accomplishments as quickly as possible. List any new ones that occur to you while you write.

Do this for each heading. Then, review your list. As you read each item, create a mental picture of yourself with that quality, talent, or accomplishment. Finally, get a

CHART #1

Recognizing My Good Qualities,
Talents, and Accomplishments

	My Good Qualities	What I Can Do Well	What I Have Accomplished
1.			
2.			
3.			
4.			
5.			
6.			
7.			
8.			
9.			
10.			
11.			
12.			
13.			
14.			
15.			

total picture for yourself with all of these qualities, talents, and accomplishments, and experience how good this feels.

Finally, to conclude, see yourself being given a large blue ribbon and pat yourself on the back to give yourself recognition. You really are first class. You've got a lot going for you and you deserve to compliment yourself for this.

2. AFFIRM YOURSELF AND YOUR TALENTS   Time: About 3 minutes

As you are what you think, if you think positively you'll feel positively. Likewise, if you think you have certain qualities and talents, that's how you'll be. Even if you don't have these characteristics now, if you think you have them, you'll develop them and your self-esteem will soar. In short, affirm what you want to get, and truly feel and believe what you affirm. This technique will help you do that.

Write down your affirmations about who you are or want to be, and about what you have or want. Choose whatever is important to you, and affirm it in the present tense, even if you don't have that thing or quality now, as we become the way we see ourselves. For example, you might affirm that:

I have an exciting, challenging job that I really enjoy.
I am making more than $5,000 this month in sales.
I am an exciting, dynamic person, and I can keep an audience excited about everything I say.
I am successful in whatever I do and now I am successfully completing a project at work.
I am prosperous and abundance comes to me.
Etc.

After you finish writing, select your most important affirmation and focus on it for about a minute. Then, close your eyes and repeat your affirmation over and over to yourself for two to three minutes. As you do this, see the statement you have written in your mind's eye. Don't just hear or see the words, but translate your message into a visual image.

Do this technique daily for about a week, and you'll notice that you feel more confident and that the things you want will start coming into your life.

For example, when one saleswoman started concentrating on a $4,000 sales figure, after averaging $2,500 to $3,000 in sales for the preceding six months, she earned nearly $5,000 in sales the following month. A management consultant who concentrated on being a successful speaker started getting paid speaking engagements for the first time, after several months of free talks for local civic groups like the Lions and Rotarians. A secretary who had found her job dull but concentrated on affirming that she had an exciting, challenging job suddenly received a special research assignment from her boss, which led eventually to a promotion to an administrative assistant, because her boss told her "I feel I can trust you to do this right."

These affirmations worked for these people because the process led to a subtle attitude change that affected the way they felt about themselves, and it led others to perceive and respond to them differently, as well. In the same way, you can make this technique work for you.

3. VISUALIZE YOURSELF AS A SUCCESS   Time: About 5 minutes

As success builds self-esteem, visualizing yourself successful helps you feel more self-assured. This process works, because not only do you make yourself more aware of opportunities to be successful, but by seeing yourself successful in the here and now, you feel what it is like to experience success. You feel more powerful, more dynamic, more directed, more self-recognition, — and all of these feelings contribute to being more confident. In effect, you're using mental imagery to convince yourself you are experiencing what you want in the here and now, and your feelings and actions respond to complement and reinforce that mental image.

I met dozens of people who did this in many workshops I attended. Typically, they attended the workshops because they were feeling uncertain about their goals in life and lacked a sense of assurance about themselves and what they were doing. But then, by focusing on and visualizing the success they wanted, they experienced transformations in their lives. Typically, they returned to the workshop or a follow-up session a week later reporting glorious changes that made them feel more powerful and confident about their abilities to create the experiences they wanted.

For example, Madge F., who worked in a dentist's office, reported having the confidence to quit and do what she really wanted—open a dress design company. Paul C., a computer programmer who was discouraged that his ideas for new software packages weren't being taken seriously by his company, felt empowered enough to push for his ideas more strongly. As a result, he gained important advocates for his idea in the marketing department.

The following exercise will give you a taste of having the type of success you want. Repeat this exercise regularly for several days to reinforce this success image and strengthen your feelings of self-esteem. Later, you can turn these feelings into reality by initiating new actions for success or by responding effectively to opportunities that come up.

Begin by deciding what sort of success is most important to you—performing well on your job, getting a larger house, starting a new company, or whatever. Next, relax, close your eyes, and see yourself realizing this goal.

Make your image of this achievement as vivid as possible, and see your success happening in the here and now. For example, if your goal is to perform well at work, see the job fully completed and done perfectly. If your goal is closing a big deal, see yourself making the pitch that results in the sale and see yourself shaking hands after signing the contract. If your goal is getting a bigger office, see yourself actually sitting in it and talking to clients.

As you visualize your success, experience the satisfaction and feeling of power this brings. Feel elated, excited, strong, powerful, fully self-confident, and in charge. Then see others coming up to you or calling to congratulate you. You feel warm and glowing as you receive their praise. They tell you how successful you are. And you feel wonderful, able to do anything you want.

See Yourself As an Abundant, Prosperous Person

Today, being abundant and prosperous goes hand in hand with success. It's a symbol of having achieved a desired goal, of gaining fame and recognition, of having power. It's a confirmation and validation for most people of having made it. Whereas the success pictured in the previous exercise represented attaining a goal, the image of prosperity in this exercise represents the rewards of that accomplishment.

Concentrating on this prosperity, in turn, helps you develop the appropriate state of mind for receiving these rewards and attracting them to you, in the same way that imagining attaining a goal creates a mind set that leads you to act or react to achieve it. Then, as you experience this mind set and concentrate on prosperity as your deserved reward, this will add to your feelings of confidence and personal power.

To feel this abundance and prosperity, use the symbols of the rewards of success that are important to you. For example, if living a rich and glamorous life style is important, use the current symbols of this life style, such as having money, owning a nice home and car, and traveling in style to interesting places. If your ideal is being a person with popularity and power, visualize images of that, such as having an entourage of people around you, giving a speech before a rapt audience of thousands, or arriving at a gala opening as the press snaps photos of your arrival. Alternatively, if you imagine yourself a philanthropist giving contributions to social causes, picture that. In short, to feel prosperous, choose the images of success you identify with, for you are using your power to visualize success to give you the success feeling.

The following five techniques will help you develop this abundant, prosperous state of mind. Then, as you go about your daily routine, think of these images and feelings from time to time, and you'll feel more confident and be more aware of and receptive to any opportunities to become successful. Within a short time, you'll find money and other forms of prosperity increasing for you, sometimes in unexpected ways.

MONEY, MONEY EVERYWHERE   Time: About 5 minutes

If money itself is an important success symbol for you, and you are interested in getting more of it—through a promotion, good stock trade, real estate sale,—this technique will make you more receptive to getting money, no matter how it comes to you.

To begin, get relaxed and close your eyes. Now see yourself sitting at home in your living room or office. You are concentrating on the word "money."

As you concentrate, suddenly, there is a knock on the door, and as you open it, a messenger enters carrying a large attaché case. This messenger, either a man or a woman, is stylishly dressed, and looks something like a banker or financial planner.

The messenger puts the attaché case on a table and gives you a key to the case, saying this is a special gift for you—a reward for all you have done. As you open the box, you see about twenty neatly arranged stacks of large bills. There are $50 bills, $100 bills, a million dollars in all.

You pick up several of the piles and run your hands through each bundle. You feel excited, energized, powerful, as you touch the bills' new crinkly surfaces. Each bundle feels thick, luxurious to the touch, and you move your fingers up and down along the edges and surfaces of each bill.

You start creating a large mountain of these bundles of bills on your table, and as you do, you run your fingers up and down this mountain. Feel it vibrate with the energy of all this money, and as you touch it, notice that the image of all the things you want to do with this money appears around the mountain.

Then, look back at the attaché case, and see that it is completely full of money again. Know, too, that you simply have to open the attaché case, and it will always be full.

So, you have all the money you want and need. You can always use it to create your mountain and visualize what you want to have, knowing you can get it. Then, feel the power and confidence that comes from having this ability.

Focus on this feeling of assurance and power for a while and enjoy it. Then, realizing you have all you want for now, close the attaché case and leave the room, knowing you can always go to this mountain to get more money, and you can always open the attaché case to get more money to build your mountain. Later, the image of the attaché case and mountain will remain with you, and whenever you want to feel powerful and abundant, you can think of it again.

MULTIPLYING YOUR ASSETS   Time: 2-3 minutes

This technique is designed to make you more aware of the possibilities for increasing your assets in the near future. As such, it is a good supplement to the *Money, Money Everywhere* technique, which makes you open and receptive, for it suggests the avenues through which you might receive more money.

To begin, take a bill from your billfold—use the largest one you have. Then, holding it before you, concentrate on it for about two minutes. As you do, notice its colors, its textures. Hold it in different ways in your hand. Meanwhile, think to yourself: "This bill is multiplying itself. There are many more of these coming my way."

Also, imagine this bill increasing in value. If it is a $1 bill, see it as a $5 bill; if it is a $5 bill, see it as $10; if it is a $10 bill, see it as $20; and so on. Meanwhile, think to yourself: "I'm not limited to what I have. I can increase the value of my money at any time."

Now, still holding the bill, ask yourself mentally: "How might more money come to me?" and get an image. For example, it might be of you in a new job, handling a new project, starting a new business, being paid for speaking to a group. Then, ask again: "How else might this come to me?" and get another image. Keep asking this question and getting images until the images stop coming freely. At the same time, feel the power you have to increase the money coming to you.

Later, you can use the information gained in this experience to make some changes in your life, if necessary, to increase your assets. Or use the feeling of confidence and power gained by the exercise to be more aware of opportunities to increase your income in everyday life.

PICTURE YOUR PROSPERITY   Time: 3-5 minutes

Whether you want a better job, a larger business, or whatever, this technique will help you focus on your goal. In turn, the positive energy you direct toward this objective will help you mobilize your inner forces to attain it.

This exercise involves creating a visual image to make your thoughts and desires more concrete, which makes them stronger and more powerful. The process works the same way as writing down goals. It makes them more real, so you're not merely casually dreaming about something, but you're working on actualizing the results you want. You're taking some steps to make sure what you want really happens.

To prepare, cut out a picture of what you want from a newspaper or magazine, or draw it. You can also cut out words or phrases that express your goals. Use an image or set of words that are as close to what you want as possible.

Now glue this picture on a sheet of cardboard. Decorate it as attractively as possible, using magic marker, drawings, and the like. Or perhaps frame it or surround it with a gold border. Finally, place a small picture of yourself in the center of this image.

Then, holding this image in front of you, concentrate on it for several minutes. See yourself getting what you want, and direct a stream of positive energy from your mind into this image.

If you feel you need additional energy, draw it into yourself from the earth or from the air around you, as previously described. Visualize the earth energy coming up through your feet and through your spine to your head, and see the energy from the air or cosmos coming down into your head. Then, direct this energy into the image.

Spend about three minutes focusing your inner forces in this way and as you do, imagine that you have achieved everything illustrated in the images or words you picture.

Afterwards, keep this picture around your house or office where you can see it from time to time as a reminder of your expected prosperity. Preferably, put it some place where others won't see it (such as in a desk drawer or closet), to better preserve the specialness of this image and give it more power.

AFFIRM YOUR PROSPERITY   Time: 1-2 minutes

To reinforce these prosperity techniques, affirm your growing abundance from time to time. You can do this wherever you are—waiting in line, on a bus, in an airplane, wherever.

In fact, when you feel especially under pressure or irritated about something, such as when a co-worker or employee doesn't do something they promised, this affirmation is a good way to perk up your spirits and help you feel secure and confident again.

Just repeat to yourself for a minute or so something like: "I am abundant," "I am prosperous." "I am rich and have all the money I need and want." When you stop, feel a flow of abundance, well-being, and power surge through you. Feel you have everything you want and can use that to do anything you wish.

FEEL CONFIDENT AND SELF-ASSURED
WHEREVER YOU ARE   Time: About 1 minute

The final step to being fully confident is feeling as if you are fully in control and in charge wherever you are. Affirming your abilities and talents, and seeing yourself as an abundant, successful person helps to give you that feeling. In addition, you can increase these powerful, in-charge feelings by using mental imagery to remind you that you are in charge.

The following technique is designed to do this by giving you the experience of being in control of wherever you are. Stay fully alert as you use this technique, which includes holding a mental image of being fully in charge of the situation. This control-of-the-room approach uses one take-charge image. You can use another image that feels comfortable for you.

Know that you can feel confident and self-assured wherever you are. To feel this way, as you enter an area, imagine a force field of powerful energy radiating out from your head to the four corners of the room. At the same time, imagine a column of energy beaming down into your head from above you and flowing down along your spine and through your feet. This column of energy makes you feel strong and solid, while the force field that radiates out from you gives you control of wherever you are.

As you walk about and talk to people, feel this energy or force move with you. It remains around you, protecting you, providing assurance and control. Also, it is constantly replenished from the energy beaming into you. Once you know this energy is around you, you no longer need to focus on it. However, should you feel your assurance or control of any situation weaken, imagine that you are sending out additional force to the four corners of the room and reexperience the strong energy from the earth and air around you flowing through you and recharging you with its strength.

 *Chapter 6*

Set Your Goals to Get What You Want

THE POWER OF SETTING GOALS

Alan G. was once an ordinary student at a small Southwestern university, and, like many students, he was broke much of the time. He wasn't sure what he wanted at school, and he sat in on his courses half-heartedly, not really certain whether to take the time to do well, because he had no overall goal or purpose.

But when he got a goal, his whole life suddenly changed, and he parlayed this sense of purpose into a quarter of a million dollars within eighteen months. He discovered his purpose unexpectedly, but once he had this purpose, he clearly visualized his goal again and again and made it happen.

The change in his life began when his roommate started on a new diet and left a few cans of his special diet drink around the room. Alan noticed that some of his roommate's friends dropped by from time to time to borrow cans of the drink powder, and often some of them left notes saying they had taken the cans because they needed them now. Something must be going on, Alan thought, and he decided that if there was so much interest in the drink, then he would try becoming a distributor.

He did so, and soon he decided that this was what he wanted to do—build up a large business based on distributing this diet that was proving so popular at school. Thus, with only a few dollars in his pocket, a carton of diet drink, and an old beat-up Chevrolet, he set out for California to be near the company, so he didn't have to pay freight to get the drink.

Anyone meeting him at the time would have thought he was just another broke and crazy kid, but Alan was different—because he had a clear goal of where he was going. He could see his ultimate success so vividly that he could taste it. He worked in a large office; he had several employees working for him; he had a beautiful rambling ranch house; and he owned a gleaming Mercedes Benz.

Yet he did much more than dream about it. Holding this goal clearly before him, he worked on achieving it—and worked hard. It didn't matter to him that this goal was months away, or that he had barely enough to pay the rent now. He imagined what he needed to do to get to this goal and began doing it. He held meetings to demonstrate the product; he talked to everyone he met about the drink; he made deliveries even in the height of a raging flood. And each time he made a profit, he turned it back into getting more supply, so he could sell that, too. His was the classic Horatio Alger story, and what kept him going through the hardest times, when people he counted on didn't perform so he had to do the work himself, was his vision that he was successful here and now.

It took months of work before his vision started to be realized. But then, gradually, his efforts toward his goal started to pay off—a check for a few hundred one month; a check for $800 the next; a check for $1,500 after that. And then, suddenly, he could see it happening as the checks went up and up each month—$2,400, $4,700, $7,900, $12,000— soon he was averaging $16,000 a month or more, and by the end of eighteen months, he had accumulated approximately $250,000.

"It's a heady feeling," he told me, "to go from having almost nothing to having all the money I need to do what I want. And I credit it all to having a focus and concentrating on getting exactly what I wanted. Also, I had the conviction that I could do it. In college, I was just drifting— but then I had a sense of purpose and knew what I wanted to do."

Goal Setting Meant Marriage and Career for Sarah J.

Another person who discovered the power of setting goals was Sarah J. She operated a small specialty foods business out of her home and was involved in both selling to retail customers and finding distributors to sell her product for her. She had been involved in a number of small businesses before this, but she had approached them only half-heartedly, and her results showed this. She spent a few hours a day when she "felt like it," calling a few prospective customers for the particular product she was pushing—beauty products one month, health products another—and she made a few sales, but nothing major. She lacked the commitment and drive to be really effective.

However, like Alan, she discovered the power of setting goals. She went to an introductory meeting for a new foods program, and at this meeting, the group leader talked about the importance of goal setting. He showed what some people in the company who had made a serious commitment had earned—monthly checks of $4,000, $6,000, $7,000, some as high as $24,000. Sarah was impressed.

As a result, she sat down that night and did some serious thinking. What did she really want out of life for herself? What skills did she need to achieve this? Could she commit herself seriously to focusing on a single goal? Could she devote herself to spending a certain amount of time each day going for that objective?

After visualizing what she was doing with her life now and where she wanted to be, she decided she could make that commitment. "In fact," she told me later, "I realized I wanted to have a firm commitment with the man I was currently dating, and as a result, within two months, we decided to get married and go into the food business together."

At first, they both took part-time jobs to support themselves while they were getting the business started. But after about nine months, they were earning enough from the business that they could do it full time. "We set up our goals each week for how much we wanted to sell and how many people we needed to talk to about the product or business to do this, and then we went out to achieve this goal."

How Mary F. Used Goal-Setting Techniques to Get a Promotion

Similarly, Mary F. used goal-setting techniques to get a promotion on her job. She had been working as a secretary in a large advertising agency and was determined to become a copywriter, although her employer was not encouraging. She had no experience, and the agency was only hiring experienced copywriters.

But, instead of taking no for an answer, she focused on what she wanted. She saw herself working in the copy department and concentrated on what she needed to do to get there. Soon after she began doing this, she learned that the agency was preparing a bid for a new account, and it suddenly came to her—submit a sample advertising campaign to the copy chief organizing this effort. Thus, on her own time, she used her powers of visualization to come up with some ideas for this presentation, and she worked up a storyboard and wrote copy based on the vision that came to her when she concentrated. When the copy chief saw these, he was impressed and he showed her ideas to the staff working on the project; they incorporated some of these ideas in their sample campaign, and when the group got the project, they added her to the staff as an assistant copywriter.

I have met many other people like Alan, Sarah, and Mary, who have used mind power techniques to determine their goals, commit themselves to achieving them, and then put their commitment into action. It doesn't matter what the goals are. The key is having a goal that is realistic and achievable, imagining that the goal is achieved, determining the steps to achieve it, and finally acting with a firm commitment and assurance to attain that goal.

The following techniques will help you select your own goals, decide what you need to do, and begin the process of attaining them.

DECIDING WHAT YOU WANT

If you already know what you want and have a realistic goal, you can skip this section. But many people don't know—or they want so many things there is no way they will get anything because they lack focus. Then, too, some people set up unrealistic, impossible goals for themselves, which are really more like pipe dreams—something to wish for, but not something to take seriously—such as living the lavish life of a movie star in Beverly Hills, when, in fact, one is a quiet, private type of person.

Another problem many people have is being too vague about what they want, such as saying in general terms: "I'd like to have a million dollars." Another obstacle occurs when people don't feel an intense conviction that they really want something. Also, some people don't prioritize what they want or determine how important gaining something is to them, so they diffuse their energy by going after the less important things as well, rather than concentrating on what they truly desire.

In short, to get what you want you have to begin by knowing what this is and to know this you must:

- have a clear, specific picture of what you want (for example, I want to live in a house renting for about $1,000 in a specific area of the city).

CHART #2   Writing to Discover What I Want

1. What are some things I want right now?

2. What are some things I want in 3 months? 6 months? 1 year? 5 years?

3. What would I like to achieve within the week?

4. What would I like to achieve with 1 month? 3 months? 6 months? 1 year?

5. What is my most important goal or goals?

6. Why is this goal important to me?

7. What other questions are important to me now?

8. Question #1: _____

9. Question #2: _____

10. Question #3: _____

- determine how important your various goals are to you, and focus on your more important goals first (at most, go for two or three goals at the same time).
- determine if your goals are realistically achievable for you.
- infuse your goal with your feeling of conviction that you really want it and are willing to do what it takes to get it.

These next few techniques are designed to help you better know yourself, so you can make the appropriate decisions about setting your goals.

---

1. VISUALIZE THE INNER YOU AND LEARN WHAT YOU WANT
Time: 10-15 minutes

The purpose of this technique is to discover more clearly who you really are, by peeling yourself down to your core like an onion. When you have this information, you are in a better position to know that you truly want a particular goal, rather than adopting it because this is something that people around you want. In other words, you are seeking the "true you," because this is the you that will make the commitment to do what it takes to achieve this goal. But first this you has to be convinced enough of the value of the goal to make the commitment.

To use this onion peeling technique, get very relaxed and, preferably, lie down. The following description can be used as a guide—simply read it to yourself first; then use it as a basic scenario. Or read it into a tape and replay to direct your experience.

See yourself as a large onion, composed of many layers. On the outside, there is a slightly brownish shell. It peels off easily. But as you go down, the layers get thicker and thicker, and whiter and whiter. Now begin to peel, starting with the thin outer layer. This is your outer self. It is the layer of your outer masks and social behavior. As you peel off this layer, see an image representing the other you emerge. Simply observe this image and note it. It doesn't matter now what it means.

Now peel off the next layer. This is the layer of your physical body. It is your material, physical layer. As you peel it off, see another image representing you as your body appears. Again, just observe and note it.

Next, peel off your middle layer. This is the layer of your intellect, which contains your thoughts. Observe whatever comes to you now. Now down to your fourth layer—the one next to your center. This layer is much thicker and whiter than the others. It is the layer representing your emotions. It contains your feelings. Observe the image that comes.

Finally, see yourself peeling apart the last layers and coming down to your core. Now you have arrived at your inner being or spiritual self. Here your inner aspirations reside. Notice the image of you that emerges now.

Then, in your mind's eye, see a picture of all five images, one on top of the other. What do you notice? Are they similar? Different? Which do you especially like? Are there any you don't? Do the images seem connected? Or if not, is there anything you can do to make them more consistent or interconnected?

Now focus on the inner level that represents your inner self or being, and ask yourself: "What do I really want? What will really satisfy me? What can I commit myself to wholeheartedly?"

Then, observe what images or ideas come. If you get pictures, words, or feelings you don't fully understand, ask yourself what these images or ideas mean, and again relax and be open to whatever comes. You may get full clarification when you are in this relaxed state, or if not, remember these impressions and think about what they mean to you after the experience is over.

When you are done, count backwards from ten, and when you reach one, open your eyes, feeling refreshed and back in the room. Now, if you wish, record any insights you have gained about yourself.

2. USE AUTOMATIC WRITING TO DISCOVER WHAT YOU WANT   Time: 10-15 minutes

An alternate approach to learning what you want is using automatic writing. This is a way of letting go of your conscious mind to let your thoughts flow more spontaneously. Then you can ask yourself questions about anything, including what you want. In addition, you can use this technique to ask further questions, as discussed in the next section, about how to attain your goals once you decide what they are.

To start the process, take a sheet of paper and write down the question you want answered, such as, "What Do I Want?" "What Do I Want to Achieve?" "What is My Most Important Goal or Goals?" "Why is This Goal Important to Me?"

Next close your eyes and meditate on this question for a few minutes. Notice any images, words, or phrases that come. But don't try to analyze or understand them yet. After you finish concentrating, write down these images and impressions.

Next, still in this relaxed state, ask yourself the same question over and over. Phrase it to emphasize that you are probing for the deepest answers. For example: "What Do I Want?" "What Do I Really Want?" "What do I *Really* Want?" Write down the first answer to each question that pops into your head.

Keep asking the same question until the answers stop coming spontaneously. Then review all your responses. Pay special attention to the last ones, as these should come from the deepest part of you. What do these answers tell you about you and the goals you want? How important are these goals? How committed are you to achieving them? How certain are you that these are realistic goals? How convinced are you that you will do what is necessary to attain them?

DECIDING IF YOUR GOALS ARE REALISTIC AND BECOMING CONVINCED WHAT YOU WANT CAN AND WILL OCCUR

Beside setting a clear goal, you also need to create a goal you can realistically achieve, and you must be truly convinced you can obtain it. One way to gain this assurance is to look into your probable future to determine what you are likely to expect.

The future is probable, because when you look ahead, you will see likely alternatives. Any of these might happen, but the future isn't fixed. You always have the power to change what you see if you wish to have something else happen. Or you can work toward creating what you see.

To some extent, the future you perceive represents a projection based on what is happening to you now. If you keep doing what you are doing, certain futures are more likely. On the other hand, you can change the probabilities yourself by changing what you are doing now. In other words, you can alter your present to change your future. In turn, when you have a general sense of what is likely to happen, you are in a better position to plan and develop a series of steps to achieve your goals.

The following series of exercises is designed to help you look ahead and see what is likely to occur. Then, you can decide if that is what you want or not and act accordingly.

---

1. WHERE AM I LIKELY TO BE?   Time: About 5 minutes

Get relaxed using any relaxation technique and close your eyes. Then, imagine that you are drawing energy in from all around you, and feel this energy coming in and infusing you with wisdom and clarity. You might imagine you are drawing energy from the earth up from your feet and energy from the air down through your head. Experience this energy coming together within your body as a brilliant beam of light, which vitalizes your whole being and helps you feel wise and all knowing.

Now, as the energy continues to flow through you, look around. You are in a train station. But it is a unique station: the train consists of six sleek silver cars that run on a monorail and their destination is a time, not a place. You can see this on the sign on the station platform. It says "Destination: The Future."

This train will take you there. So climb on one of the cars, and decide where in the future you want to go. Two months ahead, six months, one year, two years, or more? The train can travel up to ten years ahead.

Now lean back and go. The ride is very smooth and fast. Places, people, train stations whizz by quickly like a blur. You barely see them as you pass. And then you are there.

Now step out and into future time. Notice what or who is around you. What are you doing? Is this what you want to do? Ask yourself any questions you want about what your life is like now. Then wait for each answer.

When you have learned all you want, step back into the train. If you wish, travel onward to another time period. Or return to the present and come back to normal consciousness.

After this experience, ask yourself questions about the future you have seen. How do you feel about this future? Do you want this? If so, you can think about what you can do to best achieve this goal. If not, you need to consider creating an alternate future and changing your present, so you can create the kind of future you really want.

2. WHAT IS LIKELY TO HAPPEN?   Time: 3-5 minutes

This technique is useful both in thinking about long-term goals and assessing the outcome of everyday activities. You ask yourself what is likely to happen tomorrow, next month, next year—any time frame you want to know about. Then, if you like what is probable, you can either relax or do what is necessary to make that happen. Or you can intervene to find a new, more desirable direction.

Get relaxed and close your eyes to begin the process. Once you feel ready, visualize yourself in a small dark room. You are seated in a large comfortable chair in front of a small table. One small light glows in the room and casts its light on the table. There you see a large crystal ball that is round and firm—or if you prefer, see a large computer screen that is lit up.

Now, put your hands around the crystal or on the computer console. As you do so, feel the energy of whatever you are touching throb with power. It's like a radio receiver, receiving energy waves from the universe. Whenever you ask it a question, it will light up with an image or you will hear a voice with your answer.

Now ask your question. What will happen at a certain time? What will the outcome of something be? Then wait for your answer. It will appear as an image in the crystal ball or on the screen, or a voice will speak to you. When that image or voice fades, ask additional questions if you wish. When you finish, the image of the crystal ball or computer console will fade.

Afterward, write down your prediction and think about it. Is this something you want? If not, what can you do to change it?

3. HOW REALISTIC ARE MY GOALS?   Time: 1-2 minutes

This is a quick technique to assess the practicality of your goals, after you have decided what you want or have considered what is likely to happen. This technique is especially useful when you either hope something will happen or are afraid something will and aren't sure.

For example, suppose you are hoping for a new promotion or a new job. You might ask if you are likely to get it. Or suppose you are thinking about moving and aren't sure if you can afford to move to a nicer place with a higher rent. You think you want it, but you don't know if this is a realistic goal for now. This technique can help you decide.

There are two versions of this technique. Use the approach that feels more comfortable for you. In one, you use the crystal ball or computer screen method just described to ask yes and no questions. In the other, you ask your body for yes and no cues.

The Crystal Ball/Computer Screen Technique. This approach begins like the "What is Likely to Happen?" technique just described. You imagine a crystal ball or computer screen before you and ask a question, such as: "Will I get the job?" "Should I take the more expensive apartment?" However, instead of seeing an image or hearing a voice with a message for your answer, you simply see or hear the words "yes," "no," "maybe," or "not sure."

The Body Cues Technique. This technique takes a little practice to develop accuracy. But once you are accustomed to it, you'll be able to get your answer in a few seconds. Essentially, what you are doing is reading your own body for answers, as your body holds the key to your subconscious. But first you have to train your body to give those cues.

Initially, you'll need to physically move your body to get your answers. However, after some practice you can visualize these bodily movements in your mind. Or you can develop a voice inside you to answer for your body.

To get your body accustomed to giving you answers, use the following procedure to get your responses physically. Later, go through this process in your mind.

Stand straight and imagine your body as a pendulum. Now sway backward and forward. That means "yes." Sway to the right and to the left. That means "no." Sway in a circular motion. That means you are not sure or can't answer now.

Practice these motions until you are familiar with the signals. Then ask yourself some simple yes-no questions to which you know the answer. Your body should respond with the appropriate swaying motion. Once it does consistently, you are ready to begin asking it for answers.

Now ask your questions about your goals as yes-no questions, and learn either if your goals are realistic or if they are in your best interest. For example, ask:

"Is my goal (state it clearly) likely to happen?"
"Is this a realistic goal to have at this time?"

Or ask:

"Should I have this goal?"
"Is this a beneficial goal for me to pursue at this time?"

After you ask each question, observe how your body responds—with a yes motion, a no, or a maybe. With practice, you should get clear yesses or nos. Once you do, you can decide whether to act accordingly.

If you get a lot of circular motions (maybes) or get alternating yesses and nos to the same question, you may not be asking the question clearly, or your personality may be getting in the way. To find out, simply ask: "Is my question unclear?" Or "Is my personality getting in the way?" If so, either clarify or reframe your question.

PRIORITIZING YOUR GOALS

If you have developed a number of goals that you can realistically achieve, you need to decide how relatively important these goals are to you, as you can only focus effectively on at most a few goals at a time. Also, it is often helpful to have an overall goal that is most important to you, as this helps to give you a sense of direction and focus. Then, with this primary orientation you can concentrate your energy on achieving your purpose.

You might think of this process as concentrating your energy like a laser beam, as compared to the scattered light emitted by a flashlight. Scattered light will reach the same target, but it is diffuse, whereas the laser beam will pierce right through with its intense burning light.

For example, if you're a manager at work, your primary goal might be to motivate your group to achieve a certain level of productivity. If you're an employee, your goal might be to complete a series of tasks effectively so you are in line for a promotion. Or if you have your own business, your goal might be to attain a certain volume of business and do whatever is necessary to stimulate that volume.

If you aren't already clear on the relative importance of your goals, this technique will help you rate your goals and prioritize them.

WHAT ARE MY MOST IMPORTANT GOALS?   Time: 5-10 minutes

Take a sheet of paper and a pencil, and write these headings across the top: *My Goals, Their Importance to Me, My Most Important Goals,* and *Rating My Most Important Goals.* Next draw a line between each of these headings, so you have four columns.

Now get calm and relaxed using any method that works for you. You want to be in a quiet, meditative frame of mind to do this process.

Then, as quickly as you can, write down all your goals. Don't try to think about them or judge them. Some goals may be very general, some very specific, some long-term, some short-term. It doesn't matter. Just write down whatever comes to you. Probably, you will write down some of the goals you have already come up with in previous exercises. But you may find that other goals surface, too. Keep going until you feel yourself slowing down. Then concentrate for perhaps another minute until you feel finished.

Now look down this list quickly and rate each goal in order, based on how important it is to you, using a rating scale of 10 (most important) to 0 (least important). Put down the first impression that comes to mind as you do this in the second column on the same line as that goal. Don't think about your reasons for giving a particular rating—just let your inner self respond intuitively. Then your immediate response will give you an accurate picture of how important that goal is to you.

Next, list your goals with the highest rating in the third column. Start with any 10s and list them, next any 9s, and so on, until you have written down three or more goals. Stop after you have listed at least three goals—just be sure to include all the goals in the last numerical category listed.

Finally, look at this list of your most important goals, and as quickly as you can, rank them in order, from 1 (most important) to 3. Don't worry about the other goals on your list. You are interested in the three most important goals to you. Also, don't try to think as you rank your goals. Just react as quickly as possible to tap your inner feelings.

The result of this exercise should be discovering the goal that is most important to you, so you can focus on what you need to do to achieve this goal. Then, if you have additional time to devote to working on your goals, you can try to attain goals 2 or 3, too. But put your emphasis on goal 1. This is your most important goal—so that's what you should go after accomplishing first.

CHART #3

Discovering My Most Important Goals

My Goals	Their Importance to Me	My Most Important Goals	Rating My Most Important Goals

DEVELOPING THE CONVICTION YOU WILL ACHIEVE YOUR GOAL

Once you are clear what you want, know it is realistic, and are certain this is your most important goal, you need to regularly energize it with your conviction that you will achieve this goal, and you will do what is necessary to achieve it.

For example, I did this recently in finding a new place to live that I could also use as as office and meeting facility for my business. I focused very clearly on what I wanted; got a picture of where in San Francisco I wanted to be; even picked out a section of several blocks where I wanted to move; and repeatedly visualized myself finding a place and living there. Furthermore, I imagined moving in as of a certain date, but not before, as I was paying rent somewhere else until then. Within three days of looking, I found exactly the place I wanted, much like Ann S. described in an earlier chapter. The flat I located had just come on the market. I saw a sign on the street as I drove through the area looking at other places. I was the second person to look at it, and the first person who liked it—a group of psychiatrists who wanted an office for their clients—took the flat upstairs.

Furthermore, although the flat cost almost twice as much as I had ever paid for a residence and business place, I was totally convinced that this was the right place and that I would find the extra income to pay for it. And I soon did by finding new creative uses for the property—such as renting it out to other people for meetings and for shared office use.

In short, you need to be fully convinced that you will get what you want and will find the method to do so. Then, you will!

The following exercise is designed to help you develop this feeling of conviction.

BECOMING CONVINCED   Time: 3-5 minutes

Get relaxed and close your eyes. Find a few minutes during the day when you can do this, or perhaps do this when you are drifting off to sleep in the morning or right after you wake up.

Then, concentrate with all your attention on realizing your goal. See your goal already achieved. For example, if it is a material possession, see yourself owning it and enjoying it. If it is a new job or business, see yourself in your new role. If it is a new place, see yourself in this new environment.

Make your images of your goal as clear as possible. Be aware of everything you see—colors, objects, people, rooms, furnishings, and so on. Listen to what you hear around you—sounds, voices, conversations. Touch objects around you. Notice anything you smell, taste, sense moving, and so forth.

In short, experience achieving your goal as fully as possible. In fact, you might imagine yourself as the director of a movie, on location, shaping everything as you want it right now!

Then, as you see this goal achieved very vividly, say to yourself: "I will achieve this goal. I will do what is necessary to get it. This goal is completely possible. I just need to act to get it, and it will happen now!"

Finally, end this visualization and return to normal consciousness feeling totally convinced and certain you will get what you want. This feeling will stay with you during the day and will help you take the necessary steps to achieve your goal.

DETERMINING THE STEPS TO YOUR GOAL

To attain an overall goal—such as getting a new job, promotion, or certain sum of money—you need to break it down into specific objectives or steps to be accomplished, and you need to be aware of what kind of resources you might need along the way.

For example, if you are seeking a new job, some of the things that may be required are:

- a new wardrobe that is more suited to the role you wish to acquire; if you wear the new clothes now, the officers of the company are more likely to see you in a new way and are therefore more likely to give you a promotion;
- a class to brush up on some of the skills needed for the job;
- an improved relationship with a co-worker with whom you are having some problems.

If you are thinking of expanding your business, maybe you need to take some of the following steps:

- doing a location study to determine the best place to move;
- reviewing your present employees' skills to determine who might be able to take on new management responsibilities;
- writing up a loan application with supporting materials to show you have a business plan that is likely to be profitable.

You also need to work out the sequence of what you will do when and prioritize each of the activities in your plan. Then, if you find you can't do everything you wish, you can drop out the activities with a lower priority.

The following techniques will help you decide what you need to do, the resources you require to do this, how to order these activities, and how to prioritize these plans, so you can carry out your action plan most efficiently.

DECIDING ON THE STEPS TO MY GOAL   Time: 10-15 minutes

First, get a sheet of paper and a pencil and write the goal you want to accomplish on top. Next make four columns entitled: What I Need to Do:, Resources I Need:, Order of Execution:, *and* Importance of Activity.

Then, with this paper before you, take some time to get relaxed and focused. Once you feel completely calm and in a meditative frame of mind, begin.

Start by thinking of all the things you need to do to reach your goal. Don't try to judge how important these activities are. Just write down everything that comes to you in the first column: What I Need to Do. *Leave a few lines between each activity, so you can fill in the resources list in the next column. Keep brainstorming and coming up with ideas until you feel finished.*

Next go to the second column: Resources I Need. *Now look at each thing you need to do, and next to it, list any resources necessary. Again, don't try to judge or evaluate your thoughts. Just write them down. Keep going until you feel finished with each one—and if you don't need anything special for a particular activity, go on to the next.*

Now go to the third column: Order of Execution, *where you will number the activities listed in column 1 in sequence. Begin with what you should do first; then number the second, the third, and so forth. If you're not sure of the order or feel you will do some activities around the same time, give them the same number.*

Finally, go to the last column: Importance of Activity. *Again, look at the activities in column 1, and as quickly as possible, rate them as to their importance according to A (very important), B (important), and C (do if possible).*

When you are done, return to your everyday state of consciousness.

CHART #4

Deciding the Steps To My Goal

What I Need to Do	Resources I Need	Order of Execution (1, 2, etc.)	Importance of Activity (A, B, or C)

Now take the information you have acquired to make up an activities list for yourself. List the goal you are going to achieve at the top of the page (such as, a promotion at work; doubling the size of my business). Then, in order, using the numbers you have listed in column 3, write down the activities you plan to do and the resources you need to do them. Next to each one, write the letter indicating the importance of this activity.

For instance, if you are seeking a promotion. your goals list might look something like this:

1. Sign up for a class on word processing   A
   Resources needed: $200 class fee

2. Get some new clothes to present a better image   A
   Resources needed: Wardrobe consultant for advice
                                   $250 for wardrobe consultant
                                   $2,000 for new clothes

3. Improve relationship with co-worker   B
   Resources needed: Make the first move in saying
                                   good morning
                                   Start a casual conversation
                                   Find out about her interests

If you are considering a business expansion, you might list some of the following activities:

1. Write up a business plan   A
   Resources needed: Writer to assist me
                                   Business records of past performance
                                   Clear picture of where I want my
                                   business to be

2. Go to bank for business loan   A
   Resources needed: Business plan
                                   Financial statement

3. Location study to determine where to move   B
   Resources needed: Management firm to do study
                                   $1,000 to 2,000 for study

4. Assessing skills of current employees to make
   promotion decisions   A
   Resources needed: Review of employee records
                                   Interviews with key employees

CHART #5

Putting My Goals Into Action

Goal #	Goal and Resources Needed	Priority

START NOW!

Once you know your goal, are committed to achieving it, and know what you need to do to get it, the final step is START NOW!

Perhaps use some of the energy raising techniques described earlier in Chapter 4 to infuse yourself with the energy you need to get started with enthusiasm. Maybe use some of the techniques described in Chapter 5 to build your confidence that you will attain your goal.

And then, with conviction, commitment, and a one-pointed focus, begin the process of getting what you want. Know you'll get it. Believe you can do it. Do what is necessary to accomplish your goal. And you will!

That is the magic of these mind power techniques. By thinking, imagining, and knowing what you want, you will mobilize yourself to take the appropriate actions to get it. In effect, you are creating the situation necessary to attain what you desire. The outcome you want starts within you!

 *Chapter 7*

Increase Your Skills and Creativity

THE EFFECTS OF MENTAL IMAGERY ON PERFORMANCE

Is there some skill you want to develop to help you at work, such as word processing, giving talks, or communicating better at meetings? Do you want to become more creative and productive?

These mind power techniques can help you improve in both areas. To develop any skill, use your power to create mental imagery to practice in your mind. And to increase creativity, use your mind powers to visualize or think about new ways of doing things.

The power of the mind to affect performance has become widely recognized by researchers and trainers. For example, thousands of sports figures use mental imagery techniques to develop and perfect their skills and win competitions. They mentally practice their sport to supplement their real practice and before a big competition they psyche themselves up by visualizing themselves winning the game. The power of these techniques is so great that specialists in peak perform-ance, like Charles Garfield, have been working with coaches to train athletes in using imagery most effectively.

Similarly, artists, architects, writers, advertisers, and others reg-ularly use their powers of visualization to come up with ideas for creative projects.

THREE PEOPLE WHO USED MENTAL
IMAGERY TECHNIQUES EFFECTIVELY

You can apply these imagery techniques for greater success in your work and business, too. For whatever skill you want to develop, however you want to apply your creativity, these techniques will help.

Sarah H. Overcame Her Fear of Speaking to
Realize Her Career Goals

For example, Sarah H., now a seminar leader and trainer, used these methods to overcome her fear of speaking, so she could become a college teacher and later move into the training field. All her life she had felt held back by this fear, and when she became a graduate student in political science, she decided she had to do something to improve her speaking abilities if she was ever going to realize her dream of being a college professor and doing research. This was an important goal for her because she liked being in an educational atmosphere and always discovering new things. She enjoyed the interaction in seminars, and she had dozens of ideas for research projects she wanted to conduct. Yet, when it came to being in front of a large group of students or anyone else, she was painfully shy, and she knew she had to overcome this to get ahead. As she knew, to become a seminar leader or researcher in her field, she first had to teach undergraduate classes and to get the experience for this, she first had to perform successfully as a teaching assistant.

The prospect of doing this frightened her, although she realized she had to do it. Thus, she began taking the first steps to overcome her fears using a combination of actual practice and mind power techniques. To gain practice at being in front of a group, she joined Toastmasters International, a self-help group for speakers, the summer before her first year in graduate school. As a member, she spent a few minutes each week getting up in front of the group and talking impromptu on some subject. Also, she put together a few simple speeches on her interests and background.

At the same time, she spent a few minutes each day visualizing herself in the role she wanted. She imagined herself getting up in front of her class, introducing the schedule for the year, and going over the professor's lecture. She imagined herself being calm, confident, and completely knowledgeable. She imagined the students responding enthusiastically. They raised their hands, asked questions, and offered opinions; and she felt completely in charge. The result of this regimen was that a few weeks later, when the quarter started, she went into the classroom feeling completely in control. She had developed a belief from her practice that she could do it, and when she began teaching the class, she felt like she could almost go into automatic, as she had practiced so many times in her mind. Thus, now, when she actually did what she imagined, she already knew what to do.

In turn, she conveyed that sense of knowing and being in charge to her students, and the class went much as she had imagined. She presented the material successfully; she remembered the main points she wanted to discuss; and the old fear of performing properly was gone. She had acquired that sense of knowing and assurance that comes from practice—even if much of that practice was in her mind.

How Jerry S. Used Mind Power to Increase His Income

Similarly, Jerry S. used his powers of visualization to become a better salesman and increase his income. He tried his hand at various sales jobs after leaving college, and eventually he ended up going through a real estate training program and selling real estate for a large company. But he was disappointed by his lackluster performance compared to the other salespeople. He was only making a few sales a month and experiencing a rejection rate of about ninety-five percent, whereas some of the company's top performers were averaging four or five sales and closing about ten to fifteen percent of the people they worked with.

Then, at a luncheon meeting of his sales group, he heard a speaker talk about the power of creative visualization and thought he would give it a try. Accordingly, he spend about fifteen minutes each day before he went to bed visualizing himself giving a sales pitch to his prospects. He saw himself taking them to a house, giving them an enthusiastic build-up on the way, and listening to what they wanted. Also, he imagined arriving at the house, showing the prospects around, and telling them about the benefits they would find especially appealing.

Within a few days, Jerry noticed a powerful effect. He found he gave his sales talk about the house more convincingly. He seemed to know exactly what to say and when, because he had already practiced in his mind. Also, he felt more enthusiastic as he spoke, as he had felt this enthusiasm when he practiced. In turn, his prospects were more responsive. They appeared to be more reassured by what he said, felt he was more knowledgeable, and trusted his claims more. Their more favorable attitude showed in his sales—four in the first month after he started practicing these techniques.

Other people I know have become more creative using these methods. For example, Sally G., who had been an ordinary housewife, began using her powers of visualization to invent dolls, and eventually she expanded this side interest into a doll design company. She develops her ideas by visualizing the doll in her mind, and sketching what she sees.

Mind Power Helped Dan R. Find Creative Solutions to Company Problems

Dan R., an organizational development specialist, found the mind power techniques for changing things useful for creating new organizational structures. His job was to go into a company or association having problems and interview employees to learn their views of what was wrong. At one time, he tried finding a solution by using this information in a completely logical, analytical way. But then he found it more effective to use his intuitive or creative powers as well in finding a solution. To do so, he closed his eyes, saw the problem on a screen in front of himself, and began projecting a series of alternate company arrangements on the screen, until he suddenly sensed that one of the alternatives felt exactly right.

I constantly use these techniques to come up with new ideas. For instance, many clients come to me for information on marketing, and after they have described their situations, I put myself on auto-pilot and use my powers of mental imagery to come up with as many feasible alternatives as I can think of for each company. Say the company wants to promote a new specialty food product. I immediately ask myself some questions, such as: "Who would like this? What are some novel ways to serve this? What types of slogans could express the main benefits of this product?"

Then—and this is the key—after framing the question, I don't try to answer it logically. I just let my mind go and wait for the answers to come. If I'm alone I might say the answers into a tape recorder or write them down as they pop into my mind; or if I am with a client, I simply say whatever I'm thinking. Some of the ideas will be good; some won't be; but the key is not to interrupt the creative process—just let the inner mental imagery process flow freely.

Afterward, when this process slows down or stops, I critically assess each alternative. This approach is much like the brainstorming process in a group setting, where each person shouts out ideas as they come up and someone else keeps a record, so the group can evaluate the ideas later. However, in this case, I am brainstorming on my own, using that intuitive power we all have to generate the ideas that I will evaluate later.

USING MIND POWER TECHNIQUES TO INCREASE YOUR SKILLS

The key to increasing your skills with mind power techniques is rehearsing what you want to learn in your mind. By doing so, you reinforce what you have learned through physical practice, as the mind doesn't clearly distinguish between what you do in reality and what you do mentally. The result is that you can cut down on actual practice time and speed up the time you need to improve. Furthermore, by working with the skill you want to acquire in your mind, you can see yourself performing it perfectly, which provides an ideal model you can strive to achieve when you perform the activity in reality.

Using the ideal model is crucial for your success. You need to see yourself doing the skill perfectly to attain this goal. Otherwise, if you make mistakes in your mental practice, you'll make the same mistakes in the real world. So to improve your typing skills, see yourself hitting every key correctly; to improve your sales ability, see yourself making a perfect presentation, asking the right questions, and closing each sale. If a mistake should appear as you visualize, simply imagine yourself quickly correcting it. You want to create an image of perfection to influence what you do in real life.

The following visualizations will give you some examples of how to use the process. However, as the skill you seek to acquire and your present level of training will vary for each person, use the principles underlying these examples to create your own visualizations for the skill you want to acquire.

When you do this, keep these major points in mind:

- Initially select a method you have learned to do physically or have seen someone else use and visualize this in your mind. For instance, if you have just learned some basic procedures for operating a word processor, see yourself going through these procedures in your mind. Or if you have seen someone give an impressive speech, imagine yourself giving a talk using the same approach as this speaker.

- See yourself doing whatever you do correctly and effectively, as the image in your mind will eventually translate into reality.

- Imagine yourself practicing the skills you desire as vividly as possible. Visualize the setting; see yourself or others dressed appropriately to practice that skill; notice anyone else in the environment. The more real you can make your mental experience, the more powerful it will be in translating into a real life event.

- Repeat this visualization again and again, to give it more power.

- Feel yourself becoming more skilled, confident, and assured as you practice, as this feeling will carry over into real time and will help you perform better. When you return to normal consciousness, carry this feeling of success and confidence with you.

---

1. SAMPLE SKILLS VISUALIZATION: IMPROVING YOUR SPEAKING ABILITY IN A GROUP
Time: 5-10 minutes

Close your eyes. Relax. Now see yourself in your office or in a quiet place at work. You have some time to prepare for an upcoming group meeting, and you go over what you are going to say in your mind.

You see yourself thinking of the key points you want to make. You imagine how you are going to say them and which points you will make first.

Then, you rehearse these ideas in your mind. You say them again and again to yourself, until you feel really certain of what you want to say and how to say it.

Now, feeling sure of yourself, imagine you are with that group. You enter the room feeling very confident about what you are going to say. Then, you present your arguments or comments. You do so forcefully and authoritatively, and you notice that the others are listening closely to what you say. When you are finished, they agree with you.

Then, as the conversation continues, you make additional points from time to time, and again, you know exactly when to say what you say, and you phrase it exactly the right way. In turn, the other group members highly value your ideas, and they show their approval by listening closely and praising what you say.

Continue to practice in your mind's eye for a few minutes and notice your sureness and control. Notice how much your speaking ability has improved and how much surer of yourself you are. This feeling will stay with you when you return to normal consciousness and you will notice an immediate improvement the next time you speak in a group or give a presentation.

2. SAMPLE SKILLS VISUALIZATION: IMPROVING YOUR TYPING OR WORD PROCESSING SKILL   Time: 3-5 minutes

Close your eyes. Relax. Picture yourself in your office where you normally type or use a word processor. Your typewriter or word processor is the one you usually use.

Now sit down at it, ready to type. You feel very comfortable. Scan your eyes over the letter keyboard. If you are using a typewriter, insert a sheet of paper and position it. If you are using a word processor, turn on the machine, call up the appropriate program, and use the appropriate commands to prepare the system to write.

Now, place your hands on the keyboard and begin to type. Your hands know exactly what to do, and your fingers move easily across the keys.

Imagine you are typing a particular letter or report, and see yourself striking the correct letters. Continue typing for a few minutes, and notice that you're doing so perfectly.

Later, when you actually sit down at your typewriter or word processor, you will find you can type faster with increased accuracy, and you carry a feeling of confidence and self-assurance with you.

3. CREATING YOUR OWN SKILLS VISUALIZATION   Time: 3-10 minutes

You can use the above format to create your own skills visualization. Decide what skills you want to develop, create a mental scenario where you are using that skill, and see yourself doing it perfectly.

After you have practiced several times, you will immediately begin seeing the results in your improved performance. Continue doing this visualization until you have acquired the facility you want with that skill. Once you attain this level, if you perform this skill regularly, your everyday habit reflexes will take over, and you'll be able to perform this skill automatically and effectively.

As a result, you will no longer need to practice mentally on a regular basis. However, from time to time, to polish your abilities, go over your skill in your mind. If you expect to use these skills for a particularly critical occasion, such as a big presentation to a client or keynote speech to a business group, mentally review, so you feel completely prepared and psyched up to put on your best possible performance.

USING MIND POWER TECHNIQUES TO INCREASE YOUR CREATIVITY

Everyone is naturally creative, as the essence of creativity lies in coming up with new ideas, doing things differently, and thinking of alternative approaches. People do so all the time.

Such creativity leads to new products, new business ventures, and new modes of social organization, for creativity is the basis of all social progress and change. In turn, creativity is most effective when it is channeled to respond to some significant need and when it is organized and controlled to lead to an effective, productive outcome. As Kaiser Aluminum so succinctly states in the motto, that is painted on the side of its pink cement trucks: "Find a need and fill it."

The value of these mind power techniques is they can both increase your ability to come up with new ideas and direct your creative processes so these are more effective and productive.

More specifically, these techniques are designed to help you further develop the qualities that make up creativity:

- the ability to perceive and think in innovative ways
- an openness to alternative ways of doing things

As being creative effectively is a process rather than a result, these techniques focus on helping you adopt the attitudes you need to be more creative. Then you can apply this outlook to any area you choose to express your creativity, ranging from organizing your office to coming up with ideas for new products, programs, and organizations.

The three key ways of being creative that you can apply to increasing your creativity in the workplace include:

- Seeing new uses for things

   (For example, that's how the extremely successful Post-It notes were developed. Someone came up with the wrong glue formula and the glue wasn't strong enough. But someone else thought of a new way to use that glue for temporary uses—and it turned into a million dollar business.)

- Finding new methods or materials to attain that goal

   (In this case, the famous dictum: "necessity is the mother of invention" can be especially appropriate. For instance, suppose you are having a client conference and you suddenly discover that the charts you were going to use for your presentation are in a locked office and you don't have the key. This might be a time to find an alternative way into the office—and if that doesn't work, perhaps change the presentation, so you don't need the charts.)

- Making changes in what already exists or combining what exists in new ways

    (Frequently such change is vital to keep people stimulated and excited at work. For example, people can often get bored if they have to do the same things every day, and they can get stale working with the same team of people. But if an employer juggles tasks and people around, this can get people motivated again. Even just observing the work process to recommend changes can have this effect. Employees think that someone is interested in them, and that inspires them to improve. Researchers have called this process the "Hawthorne Effect"—using intervention alone to stimulate better performance—because they first noticed the effect in a plant in Hawthorne, New Jersey.)

The more you develop your abilities in these areas, the more creative you become, and the more you can direct your creativity to be more effective in your work or business.

The following exercises are designed to help you mobilize these creative processes, so you can apply them as you wish. The examples given are merely illustrative; there are so many ways to apply your creativity, depending on your goal. The key point is that once you increase your creativity, you can apply it to be more productive in anything you want.

1. Seeing New Uses for Things

Seeing new uses for things is the essence of innovation, and there are countless benefits. You can increase the value of a tool or piece of equipment by finding new uses for it. You can reduce expenses by using some items you already have for other purposes. You can expand the market for a current product by thinking of different ways new population groups can use it. Plus, you have the potential to generate millions by discovering a novel and popular use for something, and creating a phenomenon such as the Pet Rock or Cabbage Patch Doll. The Pet Rock started out as a simple stone, but it was turned into a best-selling novelty when its designer created the concept that it was a "pet." The Cabbage Patch Doll looked like dozens of other hand-made cloth baby dolls. But it became unique through the concept of adopting it, so children and adults could think of it and relate to it as a real baby.

The following technique will get you thinking about new uses for things. You begin by imagining new uses for familiar items to get your creative juices flowing. Then, you apply the process to a specific situation, such as at work, where you really do want to discover some new uses for things.

WHAT'S NEW?   Time: 2-5 minutes

See how many new and unusual uses you can create for familiar things. Try this alone or brainstorm with a friend or associate.

Begin by getting some paper and a pencil, and writing down the names of some familiar objects. Perhaps look around your office or house and jot down the names of the objects you see. Now, for each object, write down as many uses as you can, making them as novel as possible. Feel free to change the size, shape, or color of the object. Or combine two or more objects and think up uses for them together.

For example: What can you do with a paper clip? A ruler? A pair of scissors? A lamp? What can you do with a piece of paper and a chair? A newspaper and a cup? A stapler and a picture hook? Now you take it away.

When you feel warmed up, think about any specific situations in your life in which you might want to apply this technique. For example, if your company is marketing a new product, think of all the possible uses for it, or think of all the ways the company might advertise it. Or, if you are part of a work group in your office, perhaps think of all the things the group can do besides what it is doing now. Think about what is happening in your own work environment, and come up with your own situations for brainstorming using this technique.

---

2. Finding New Methods or Materials to Attain a Goal

When you have a goal, you need to believe "I can" to reach it. Sometimes you may think you lack what you need to get there. But that's where your creativity comes in to enable you to find an alternate method or to discover resources you didn't realize you had.

For example, say you want to be hired for a particular job or project, and you are sure you can do it. But the requirements ask for some credentials or experience you don't have. If you want the assignment badly enough, come up with alternate ways to get it, such as showing the people doing the hiring that this credential isn't necessary and you can do a better job than anyone else.

How do you do this? That's where your mind powers come in to tap your creativity so you can devise convincing alternatives—such as putting together a slick proposal; completing a small part of the project on your own and doing it well; or assembling a personal portfolio on your background which includes some powerful testimonial or reference letters from important people. Then, too, when you have the interview, perhaps you need to act with supreme confidence and have an air of authority and expertise, as if you already have the job, and there's no way anyone else could be as good as you.

How Millie Got the Job Without the Right Credentials

I have a friend, Millie, who got a job as an editor on a major government project this way. She answered an ad in the local paper that asked for a journalism degree. But Millie, who has been writing for a dozen years after getting a degree in psychology, didn't let that discourage her. In her initial reply letter, she simply responded to the question about her degree by listing some of the major projects she had been involved with in the past, and later, each time the issue came up in her interview, she creatively sidestepped the issue by talking about another client she had worked for and how that experience could help her do the work needed on this project. In the end, the project leader stopped asking about her degree, looked at the portfolio she had prepared, and hired her for the job.

The process of finding new methods or materials to attain exactly what you want can work with anything. The key is to think "I can do it," whatever it is, and then determine what you need to do to accomplish it. You may be able to use what you already have on hand, although perhaps you must use it in a new way; or perhaps you need to get other resources and come up with creative ways to get them.

For example, suppose you desperately need some information about a competitor for a marketing report you are preparing for your own company. Your company's decision to make a major million dollar investment in introducing and promoting a new product is on the line. So how do you get this information, short of doing something illegal like staging an after-hours break-in? One way is to start brainstorming alternative methods; then choose the most promising one to implement. For instance, maybe you have a friend who knows someone in the company; maybe you pretend to be a freelance writer doing a story and interview someone in the company; maybe you could call some wholesalers in the industry to find out what they know.

Similarly, you might find new uses for items you have on hand to solve a problem. For instance, suppose you have to put up some pictures in the office and forgot your hammer. Well, maybe something else will work—say the bottom of a hole puncher, the heavy board under the coffee maker, the heel of your shoe. In fact, if you come up with an invention to fulfill a major need (such as an attractively decorated telephone holder, so a busy executive doesn't have to use his or her hands to talk on the phone) you, too, might become an instant millionaire.

The following technique will help you loosen up your thinking processes, so you are better able to create new approaches to achieve your goals:

NEW LOOK   Time: 3-5 minutes

See how many ways you can think of to fill a need. Brainstorm with a friend or associate if you wish. First, on a sheet of paper, make a short list of some activities you'd like to see handled another way, such as commuting to work, organizing the office staff, producing the company newsletter, or keeping burglars away.

Next, look at each activity individually, and write down as many new approaches as you can, making them as novel as possible. Imagine you have unlimited resources to create solutions and let your ideas come as quickly as possible. Later, you can evaluate these ideas and choose any you can use.

---

3. Making Changes in What Already Exists—or Combining What Exists in New Ways

Making something different or better is a key benefit of creativity and innovation—and it's the engine of progress and change. This approach has fueled modern technology and generated the race to produce better, state-of-the-art equipment in Silicon Valley and elsewhere. Likewise, you can use this approach to improve your own life at work and elsewhere.

For example, use your creativity to reorganize the office and shift responsibilities to improve the work flow and make everyone more efficient. Perhaps add several new items of decor, like wall hangings or plants, to make your office look more impressive or friendly, so clients are more receptive when they talk to you. Or maybe, if you're on a tight budget, turn some throw-away shelves and bricks into an attractive bookshelf.

In short, by applying a little change and innovation, and perhaps combining some things you already have in new ways, you can make something better, more attractive, or usable for something else...and again, you might even create a million dollar product.

However, to make the most of this change process, you must be receptive to innovation and enthusiastic about the potential of everything to change. In other words, you must both accept change and be ready to initiate it, as the situation requires, and you'll find the results pay off for you in very attractive ways—such as bigger bonuses on the job for your profitable suggestions; a promotion as your employers see your creative vision and leadership; more clients and speaking engagements from people who like your energetic, dynamic approach to life; and less stress because you are more flexible and can adjust to any situation in a world filled with change.

The following exercises are designed to limber up your mind to prime you for thinking "change." Then, when specific situations occur where change is useful, you'll be more aware of the possibilities and more creative in coming up with suggestions for effective changes.

MAKING CHANGES

Changing Things *(especially useful for developing new inventions, creating new product ideas, devising a new business plan).*

See how many changes you can make in familiar objects. Imagine the different uses these objects might have when they are changed. Perhaps brainstorm the possibilities with others.

First, make a short list of familiar objects on a sheet of paper. Choose objects that might have additional marketing possibilities if you like. Next, think of all the ways you can change each object—in size, in color, in style, in construction.

For example, how might you change a radio? Maybe you can decorate it so it has extra appeal to a certain group (like a purple radio to appeal to Prince fans; a radio shaped like a computer to appeal to people with high-tech interests). Perhaps you can add a cord so it can turn household objects on and off. Other possibilities might be adding a screen to see colors as it plays, or attaching some straps to carry it on your back.

As you brainstorm, don't expect every idea to be useful and practical. Rather, come up with as many ideas as you can as quickly as possible. Later you can eliminate the chaff and select what works.

Changing Places *(especially useful for changing landscaping and the look of your work environment).*

Discover how many changes you can make in what you see. Use a picture or look around you. To alter what you see, mentally add something, modify or rearrange things, change size relationships, or take something away.

For example, suppose you are looking at your office reception area or at a picture of it. You might mentally add some flowers to a desk; perhaps see some pictures on the wall; imagine a large reception taking place. If you look at a garden, you might imagine what the area could look like if the garden was no longer there. Likewise, you could see a large building become a small one; you could change day into night, and so on.

Visualize these changes in your mind's eye, and notice any differences in the mood of the scene or how you feel. You may notice that some settings are more stimulating and exciting than others, and they lead people to respond accordingly. For instance, in a bright cheerful office, people will be more eager to work and are likely to socialize more.

Also, don't feel you must think of only practical ideas. Just let your mental processes flow and generate as many ideas as you can. Later, you can select out what's practical and make changes accordingly.

Changing People *(especially useful for changing your own appearance to better project the image you want or changing the way you interact with your co-workers or associates.)*

Think of the many ways you can change people or yourself. You can get in practice doing this anywhere—on a bus, while waiting in line, at a cocktail party, wherever you are.

Just look around you and imagine someone you see with different features. Or look in a mirror and imagine yourself with a different look. Another possibility is to combine the features of several different people, including yourself, into one. Simply imagine what that person would look life if…and make the change.

For example, suppose a man has a mustache or a beard. How would he look without it? How about a woman with long hair? Suppose it were short? An old man? Suppose he were young? A fat woman? What if she were thin? And so on.

Similarly, if you're thinking about changing yourself, as you look in the mirror or at a picture of you, imagine how you would look with specific changes, such as: wearing different clothes, being heavier or thinner, having a different hair style, looking older or younger, with glasses and without. Later, if you come up with an image you like, you can continue to focus on it from time to time to help you make that image become reality (such as an image of yourself twenty pounds lighter).

Finally, to use this technique to influence how to interact with others, look at someone or at a picture of her, and imagine yourself saying different things to her, and see her responding in different ways. You can try this with greetings, with questions, and with making requests for her to do something. Then, if you find a particular approach gets a better response, use that in real life to improve your interaction with that person.

Making New Combinations *(especially useful for inventing new products, creating new decorative schemes for your office or home, or reorganizing a group of people).*

Increase your ability to innovate by combining familiar objects or people to create unique arrangements and organizations.

To begin, think of two or three familiar objects or people. You can have some overall goal in mind (such as creating a new product or a more effective work group) or just work on brainstorming new ideas to get your creative juices flowing and apply this approach to practical situations later.

Now, write down the names of the objects or people, and then, in your mind's eye, create a scene with these objects or people. If you have a specific purpose in mind, use that to set the scene. Otherwise, make your scene as wild and fantastic as you wish to activate your creative processes. You can make the objects or people larger or smaller than normal.

For instance, say you have chosen some Coke bottles, a sink, and some sponges and want to let your creativity go free. As you look at the bottles you might imagine them as part of a futuristic city in which the streets are paved with dishes and the houses are shaped like bottles. Or you might turn a sink and sponges into a harbor with large sponge boats. Let your imagination range completely free, and if you wish, draw a picture of your vision. This approach may seem wild and crazy at first, but the process will help you be more creative in applying your ideas to practical matters, because your ideas will come more quickly and freely.

Alternatively, if you are trying to come up with a practical result, such as a new product, you might think of how these two or three objects could be combined to do that. For instance, maybe the sponge could be placed around the middle of a bottle to create a floating bottle, so people could take their drinks into the pool without the risk of losing them.

Whatever your purpose, to use this exercise most effectively, let your inner creativity go where it will at first, and wait until later to critique your ideas.

 *Chapter 8*

How to Use Mind Power to Improve Your Memory

Improving your memory can increase your success in work and business in numerous ways. It can help you better remember tasks, so you don't forget to accomplish anything essential. And if you keep lists, a better memory can help you recall those details you weren't able to write down.

Also, a good memory can help you at cocktail parties and business networking mixers. By remembering people, you increase your chances of getting jobs and clients, and if people offer referrals, your memory can help you keep track of these contacts and what to say to them. I know many people who make·notes on business cards because they think that will help them remember; but often, their notes don't say enough and when they look at the cards a week later, they don't remember what they were supposed to do. For instance, they're not sure which person they are supposed to call and which person referred them; or they don't recall what their cryptic note "likes artwork" means.

Then, too, a better memory can help you in giving a more polished presentation or speech, telling jokes and stories that make you more interesting company, and recalling specific prices and offers, so you get a better deal. You can certainly think of dozens of other benefits. In turn, your mind power abilities can help you train your memory. I know 85 dozens of people who saw their memory powers soar once they tried using mental imagery techniques to improve their memories.

How Howard J. Learned to Remember Names and Faces

Howard J., a manager of a small printing company, used to have trouble remembering the names of people he met at cocktail and business networking parties. He would be introduced to a group of people, and, as they announced their names and occupations, he would smile and shake hands, but the person's identify would slip quickly away as he was introduced to the next person. Then, Howard began concentrating on getting an associated image for everyone he met based on some feature about him or her that stood out, such as an unusual name, striking physical feature, or noteworthy article of clothing, and he found the introductions stayed with him. One reason they did is because the process of creating an image made Howard pay more attention when he was introduced. Secondly, the image served as a reminder that made the person stand out in some way. Then, with the names and identities of these people firmly implanted in his mind, Howard was better able to carry on an informative conversation, and at times, these conversations resulted in clients or leads to other possibilities.

How Joan F. Used the Power of Her Memory to Generate Important Business Contacts

In another case, Joan F., a management consultant attending a conference in a distant city, found that using special memory techniques made the critical difference between having a very productive stay and merely attending the conference. Before Joan left, a friend had given her several telephone numbers of friends with their own small businesses in the area, and she suggested that Joan might look them up. They could show her around the city, and perhaps they might have some need for the management services Joan's company offered.

Unfortunately, Joan dropped her address book with these numbers at the airport and wasn't able to find it again. But instead of feeling frustrated and considering the situation hopeless, Joan worked on trying to recall the numbers she had written down. She visualized herself meeting with her friend, and as carefully as possible, in her mind's eye, she reconstructed the conversation leading up to her friend giving her the numbers. Then, she saw herself taking out her address book and carefully writing down the numbers, and she recalled reading back each number to her friend to make sure it was correct. The result of this process was that Joan saw the numbers leap up in her mind, and as she saw them, she quickly wrote them down again.

As it turned out, her memory was correct, and she was able to meet the people, even though she had lost her address book. Consciously, she wasn't aware of the numbers; but by tapping into her unconsciousness with her mind power abilities, Joan was able to reach into this inner awareness to extract the numbers. As a result, she met with each of the three referrals, enjoyed a gala nightclub tour with one of them, and spoke to all of them about her company, leading to the possibility of future business.

The following memory training exercises are designed to help you improve your memory in three key ways:

- You increase your ability to focus on what you want to remember.

- You work on making a clear memory picture; then file it in your mind for later recall.

- You use your powers of visualization and meditation to retrieve a memory when you want to do so.

---

1. INCREASE YOUR ABILITY TO FOCUS ON
WHAT YOU WANT TO REMEMBER   Time: 3-5 minutes

One reason many people have trouble remembering something is they don't make a clear picture of what they want to remember, because they don't pay enough attention in the beginning. Naturally, you can remember all sorts of things without being particularly attentive, as unconsciously we are absorbing information all the time and much of this stays with us, even if we are unaware of it. But, this casual absorption of information can be a hit or miss proposition.

Thus, when you're in a situation where it's particularly important to remember something, learn to pay close attention by using a memory trigger. This trigger can be almost any type of gesture or physical sign—such as bringing your thumb and forefinger together, clasping your hands so your thumbs and index finger create a spire, or raising your thumb. Whatever signal you see, it's designed to remind you that it's now time to be especially alert and listen or watch closely, so you'll remember all you can.

To create this trigger, get relaxed, perhaps close your eyes, and choose the sign you want to use. Then, make this gesture and as you do, think to yourself: "I will pay attention now. I will be very alert and aware, and I will lock this information in my memory so I can recall it later." Do this several times, and later that day (or the following day if you are beginning this exercise at night), practice using this trigger in some real-life situations. Find at least three times when you are especially interested in remembering something, and use your trigger to make yourself more alert. Meanwhile, as you make this gesture, repeat the same words to yourself as in your concentration exercises: "I will pay attention now. I will be very alert and aware, and I will lock this information in my memory so I can recall it later."

Repeat both parts of this exercise (the meditation and the real-life practice) for a week to condition yourself to associate the action you want to perform (paying attention) with the trigger (raising your thumb). Then, once this association is locked in, you don't need to continue practicing the exercise, as long as you continue regularly to use the trigger in real life.

Instead, any time you are in an important situation where you want to pay especially careful attention (such as a critical board meeting or a cocktail party with important prospective clients), use your trigger, and automatically you'll become more attentive and alert.

2. INCREASE YOUR ABILITY TO MAKE A CLEAR
   MEMORY PICTURE OR RECORDING   Time: 3-5 minutes

Besides paying attention, having a good memory depends on making a clear and sharp mental picture or recording of the person, place, or event you want to remember. But often we don't make this picture or recording very well. As a result, we may think we remember what we have seen, but we don't. Courtroom witnesses, for example, often recall an event inaccurately, although they may be positive they are correct.

Accordingly, before you can recall something properly, you must have a clear impression of it in the first place. One way to do this, once you are paying careful attention, is to think of yourself as a camera or tape recorder, taking in completely accurate pictures or recordings of what you are experiencing. Then, as you observe and listen, make your impressions like pictures or tape recordings in your mind.

It takes practice to develop this ability, and the following exercises are designed to help you do this. At first, use these exercises to get a sense of how well you already remember what you see. Then, as you practice, you'll find you can remember more and more details.

The underlying principle of these exercises is to observe some object, person, event, or setting to take a picture, or listen to a conversation or other sounds around you. Then, turn away from what you are observing or stop listening, and recall what you can. Perhaps write down what you recall. Finally, look back and ask yourself: "How much did I remember? What did I forget? What did I recall that wasn't there?"

At first, you may be surprised at how bad an observer or listener you are. But as you practice, you'll improve—and your skill at remembering will carry over into other situations, because you'll automatically start making more accurate memory pictures or recordings in your mind.

An ideal way to use these techniques is with a mental awareness trigger. Then, whenever you use that trigger, you will immediately imagine yourself as a camera or recorder and indelibly impress that scene on your mind for later recall.

The first two exercises are designed to give you some practice in perceiving like a camera or tape recorder in a private controlled setting. The final exercise is one you can use in any situation to perceive more effectively.

- Experiencing an Object. *(This will help you become more aware of what you see and help you perceive more completely and correctly).*

  Place a common object or group of objects in front of you (such as a collection of objects from your desk; a painting on your wall; an advertisement or picture from a magazine; a flower arrangement in a vase). Stare at the object or group of objects for about a minute, and notice as many things about it as you can — such as its form, texture, color, design, pattern, and so on. Be aware of how many objects there are, and catalog the names of all the objects in your mind.

  Then, remove the object, or groups of objects, so it is out of sight, but continue looking at the spot where it was, and imagine the object(s) is still there. Try to recreate what you saw with as much detail as you can.

  To check your accuracy, write down a list of what you saw. Then, look at what you observed again and see how accurate you were.

  To chart your progress each time, score the total number of observations you think were possible (this will vary with each observer), and score each of your accurate observations with a +1. Score each of your inaccurate observations with a −1. Finally, total and divide by your estimated number of total observations for your percentage rating.

  As you continue to practice with this exercise, you'll find your percentage rating will go up.

- Listening to What You Hear *(This will help you become more aware of what you hear and help you listen more completely and correctly).*

  Tape a short segment of conversation or some sounds on a tape cassette. You can record this from an ongoing conversation, from a television or radio program, or from the ambient sounds on the street around you. Tape for two to three minutes.

  Then, play back the recording and really listen. Perhaps form images in your mind as you do.

  At the end, try to recall the conversation or sounds in as much detail as possible. Additionally, try to remember what you heard in sequence as best you can.

  To check your accuracy, write down a list of what you heard. You needn't write everything down word for word, but write down enough to indicate the gist of each thought or statement. Then, play back the tape, and review how complete and accurate you were.

As in the observation exercise, to chart your progress each time, estimate the total number of sounds, statements, or phrases you think were possible (again, this will vary from observer to observer), and score each of your accurate notations with a +1. Score each of your inaccurate notations with a −1. Give yourself 10 bonus points if you got everything in sequence; 5 bonus points if you got most things in sequence. Finally, total and divide this result by your estimated number of total sounds, statements, or phrases for your percentage rating.

As you practice, your percentage rating will go up.

- Seeing Like a Camera; Listening Like a Tape Recorder *(This will help you observe or listen more accurately and completely in everyday situations).*

You can use this technique wherever you are—and it's especially ideal for parties, business networking meetings, and other important occasions where you want to be sure to remember things accurately. Also, you can use this technique to practice and sharpen up your skills when you're waiting in line, traveling in a bus, in a theater lobby at intermission, and in places where you are waiting for something to happen.

Simply imagine you are a camera and snap a picture of what you see. Or imagine you are a tape recorder picking up a conversation. Or be a sound film camera and pick up both.

Afterwards, turn away or close your eyes if convenient, and for a few seconds, focus on what you have just seen or heard. If you have taken a picture, visualize it intently in your mind's eye and concentrate. What objects or people do you see? What colors or details do you notice? What furniture is in the room? What are the people wearing? Etc.

Then, look at the scene and compare your picture with what you see now. What did you leave out? What did you add that wasn't there? What details did you observe incorrectly? The more you do this, the more complete and accurate your picture will be.

If you have tried to listen like a tape recorder, try to replay what you have heard in your mind. What did people say? What sounds did you hear around you? You won't be able to actually hear these conversations or sounds again, but at least you can get a sense of how much detail you were able to pick up. The more you practice, the more fully you will hear.

If you have imagined yourself as a sound film camera, review both the pictures and sounds.

3. INCREASE YOUR MEMORY RECALL

After you have done all you can to register a memory impression in your mind, the final step is doing everything you can to recall it. Even if you think you have forgotten, these techniques will help you release your unconscious processes, so you can dig back into your inner storage area in your unconscious to retrieve it.

Whether you want to recover a name, a telephone number, the location of an object, a route you traveled, or whatever; to recall it, recreate the original experience in your mind as realistically and dramatically as possible. If you're in a setting where you can replay the experience in reality, do it. That will help you recapture the memory.

For example, I had an experience of doing this myself the night before I sat down to write this chapter. I had parked my car to meet a friend at the theater, and as I was in a rush to get there, I forgot to look at the street signs to note where I was. I simply walked to the theater as quickly as I could, and afterwards, my friend and I walked in another direction to a restaurant, so that after we finished I was totally disoriented.

I let my friend walk off to her own car, and then I focused on replaying the route I had traveled in my mind. I saw myself driving down a certain street, turning on another street and turning again. Accordingly, I walked back to this street where I had started, followed the route I had laid out in my mind, and when I got to the end, there was my car—exactly where I had visualized it to be.

When you get accustomed to using this technique, you can do it anywhere, as I did. You don't even need to close your eyes. You can simply focus on your inner mental screen and see the image there before you.

However, when you first start using this method, you'll need a few minutes to settle down and visualize yourself in the setting, so don't expect to have instant recall right away. But after a while, with practice, the process becomes much faster, so you will soon be able to retrieve a memory in moments.

The following recall techniques will help you remember names, phone numbers, where you put an object, a route you traveled, or something you read or saw in a movie. Also, these techniques will help you recall situations and events. Plan to practice each one for a few days. Then, after you feel comfortable with it, you can use it as needed. Begin practicing each technique by getting relaxed and closing your eyes. Later, you'll find you can do it without closing your eyes.

- Recalling a Name. *Visualize the person before you. Imagine that you are meeting for the first time, and review this first meeting very closely. Be aware of who else is there, the setting, and so on. Make your picture as complete as possible. Then, greet this person as you did when you first met, and listen carefully as he or she tells you his or her name.*
- Recalling a Phone Number. *Visualize a telephone before you and see the person you are going to call near a phone, awaiting your call. Now go to your telephone and open your telephone book to the name of this person. The number will appear, or if it seems hazy, begin dialing the number, and as you dial, the number will become clear.*

  Alternatively, if you have recently written down the person's number, visualize yourself in that situation. The person is telling you his or her number and you are writing it down. Notice the setting where you are. Be aware of the type of paper you are using to write your note. Then, see yourself writing the number and repeat it to yourself as you write it. The number will appear clearly before you and you will remember it.

- Recalling Where You Put Some Object. *Think back to the last time you had that object. Where were you? What were you doing with it? Visualize yourself using that object. Then, when you are finished with it, observe what you do with it when you put it away.*

- Recalling a Route. *Visualize yourself in a car or on foot, as in your original experience. Don't try to retrace your steps backwards, but begin where you started. Now see yourself leaving from this starting point. Be aware of the surroundings you pass. Notice how far you go and look for significant route markers or landmarks. Speed up on straightaways, and pay careful attention to what is around you when you make a turn. Keep going until you get to your destination.*

- Recalling Some Information from a Book or Movie. *Visualize yourself reading the book or sitting in the movie theater. If you are reading a book, hold it in your hands and be aware of its size, shape, and texture. Begin turning pages, until you get to the page you want. Then, look down the page to the appropriate paragraph or line and read. If you are seeing a movie, experience being at the movie as intensely as possible. Sense the darkness around you; sink down in your seat. When the movie comes on the screen, see the title vividly, and fast forward the film ahead to what you want to recall. Then, slow the projector to normal speed again and watch the scene you want to see unfold. Watch the characters act and converse just as you would in a real movie, and you'll see the movie again vividly in your mind.*

- Recalling a Situation or Event. *Imagine yourself in the situation as vividly as possible. Notice the setting, the buildings, the people around you. Imagine you are a movie director and this is a scene that is about to unfold before you. You hold the script in your hands, and at your cue, the actors in the situation begin to play out the scene. You are able to notice everything, hear everything they say. If you want to move ahead faster in the scene, you simply turn a page of your script, say "cut," and direct the actors to start again in a later scene.*

Once you have gained practice in recalling the memories you want with these techniques, feel free to develop your own imagery to help you recall any situation or event. For example, maybe see yourself as an investigative reporter covering a story rather than a movie director filming a script.

The key to recall is to imagine yourself as vividly as possible in the situation you want to remember. Then, you use your mental picture or recording of that situation to stimulate your memory of the original event.

 *Chapter 9*

How to Create the Personality and Self-Image You Want

To be more successful in a career or business, it helps to have certain personality traits. To some extent, the ideal traits differ from occupation to occupation—for instance, a direct sales person needs to be an outgoing, assertive, positive, self-motivated person who takes initiative, and is persuasive and articulate, while an office worker should be especially conscientious, attentive to detail, organized, and willing to take orders. However, some traits are desirable for everyone—such as being a confident, friendly, creative, high-energy, positive person.

You need to decide the personality traits or self-image best for you and your own career or business path. Then you can decide if you have the personality or self-image you want, or determine the areas you want to develop further to get closer to your ideal.

You'll find the results can be amazing if you decide to make some changes—a job more in line with your abilities and interests; improved job performance and a higher income; and more personal power at work and at home.

Dawn F. Changed Her Self-Image for Greater Personal Success

For example, Dawn F. had been drawn into becoming a computer programmer, because she was shy and felt uncomfortable with people.

With computers though, she could work largely on her own and didn't have to worry about making an impression on others. Her employers were primarily interested in the programs she designed, not how she interacted with others.

Yet Dawn didn't feel completely happy in the computer field either. She didn't like the detail work or the intense concentration required to do a project. Rather, if she had her choice, she really wanted to overcome her shyness barrier, so she could do something involving more physical activity, variety, and contact with others.

She continued as a programmer for several years, however, feeling frustrated because her personal ambitions were out of phase with her work and her present self-image. Yet she stayed with her job and old self-picture because these were known and comfortable to her.

But then, something happened that led Dawn to start making changes. A friend learned about a new business opportunity that involved putting on home parties to sell computers, and she persuaded Dawn to join her in this venture. At first, Dawn felt nervous about trying to put on presentations and her ability to sell anything. But her friend urged her to at least try, and so Dawn began accompanying her friend to weekly sales parties. After a while, she put on a small part of these presentations, too, and in doing so, she felt a thrill of excitement at being in front of a group and a desire to get good enough to present these meetings on her own. She still felt the old awkwardness and shyness that had drawn her into the computer field, yet now she wanted to work on overcoming these feelings that had held her back.

As a result, with the help of her friend, she began changing her self-image and personality. She started thinking about the qualities she needed to develop to work with people; decided which qualities were most important so she could work on developing these first; and began imagining herself having these qualities and applying them in different situations. For example, she visualized herself in teaching a class on using computers for consulting with office managers on the best kind of system for them. Then, after seeing herself having these qualities for some time, she began actively placing herself in situations where she had to use these qualities. In one case, she joined Toastmasters International, a group dedicated to improved public speaking, to learn how to give speeches; in another case, she joined a speaker's bureau run by a woman's group to which she belonged and volunteered to give speeches. Also, she became more active selling computers through the home party plan. At the same time, she supported her efforts by using affirmations and other mind power techniques to reinforce the qualities she sought to acquire.

After about eighteen months, she had gained a firm new self-image and felt comfortable enough to quit her programming job to do what she wanted—being a full-time computer consultant and trainer. Before she had been limited by a vision of herself that held her back. But now, having changed that vision, she felt confident she could do what she wanted, and therefore did.

I have met many other people who likewise altered their personalities and self-images for greater success. A man who managed a small order processing department realized he was too abrasive in dealing with employees and worked on becoming more supportive and finding ways to give praise rather than criticism. As a result, he upped his unit's productivity, leading to a nice raise for himself. An elementary school teacher realized she tended to be too impatient and overly critical of people, which made some students resentful and caused them to lose interest in their work. To counteract this, she learned to slow down and become more patient, which resulted in a better behaved class and higher student grades.

THREE KEY STAGES TO CHANGING YOURSELF

You can similarly change yourself to become the person you want. There are three key stages to this process:

1. *Determine what you want to change or become.* Ask yourself: "How would I like to change?" For example, would you like to be more outgoing and dynamic? More warm and affectionate? More articulate? More self-assured in a group? However you want to change, your mind power abilities can help you imagine the qualities you want to eliminate and those you want to develop.

2. *Use the process of mental scripting to see yourself in your new role.* This procedure lays the groundwork for you to change, because you create a new persona or character for yourself, much like a movie director might do. Then, by rehearsing the role over and over again in your mind, you reinforce the reality of this new image. So you see yourself differently when you act in the real world, which helps you act differently as well.

3. *Put your new script in action.* Now you take the new role and actions you have created for yourself and put them into practice in real-life situations. For instance, if you have decided you want to be more outgoing and have imagined yourself being this way with your co-workers, now you do just that, keeping in mind the image of

yourself as a more outgoing friendly person who evokes positive responses from others.

The following techniques are designed to help you with each phase of this process.

HOW TO DETERMINE WHAT YOU WANT TO CHANGE OR BECOME

The process of creating a new personality or role for yourself is much like the process of getting and achieving goals described earlier—except now your goal is to become a different person. You start off by thinking about all the personality traits you want to develop, and then decide which qualities are most important to you, so you can work on achieving them first.

WHAT DO I WANT TO CHANGE OR BECOME?   Time: 5-10 minutes

To prepare, get a sheet of paper and pencil, and make two columns. At the head of one column, write down the heading: The Personality Traits I Want to Eliminate. *At the head of the second column, write down the heading:* The Personality Traits I Want to Develop.

Now, holding the paper and pencil before you, get in a relaxed frame of mind. Perhaps turn the lights down to help you concentrate—but leave on enough light so you can see to write.

Then, looking at the first column, begin brainstorming and quickly list all the traits you want to eliminate. Write down whatever pops into your mind, and don't try to judge whether it is realistically possible for you to get rid of that quality. Keep going until you have listed at least five traits or have started to slow down.

Next, turning to the second column, begin brainstorming and quickly list all the traits you want to acquire. In some cases, these may be the reverse of the traits you want to eliminate. (For instance, instead of being shy, you want to be more outgoing; instead of being impatient with people, you want to be more receptive and understanding.) That's fine. Just go ahead and list whatever comes up without trying to critique or evaluate it. Also, don't try to decide now if it's realistically possible to acquire that quality.

Again, keep going until you have listed at least five traits or have started to slow down.

When you feel finished, you are ready to prioritize the traits you want to eliminate or develop. To do this, first look down your list of traits you want to

eliminate, and for each one, come up with the complementary trait you would like to acquire and list it in the second column. For instance, if you have listed: "become less negative and critical," the complementary trait would be "become more positive and accepting." After you have listed this complementary trait, cross out the trait you want to eliminate. If you already have listed a complementary trait in the second column, simply cross off the listing in the first column.

To prioritize them, look at each quality on the list in turn, and indicate how important it is to you by using the letters: A (very important), B (important), C (nice but not that important). Write that letter down next to each quality.

Finally, look at the traits you have marked A. If you have more than one trait in this category, rank them in order of priority — 1, 2, 3, and so on. If you have no As, do the same for the Bs.

You have now established your priorities and will work on your developing your most important quality first. If you have the time and energy, add your second or third traits. But at most work on three qualities at a time. Once you feel solid about having made these part of your personality, go on to the next traits on your list in order of priority (taking all the As first in order; then the Bs; and finally the Cs). Or, if you feel you have gone through extensive changes, make a new priority list.

USING MENTAL SCRIPTING TO SEE YOURSELF IN A NEW ROLE

Once you have decided which trait or traits to develop first, the next step is using mental scripting to develop them. In mental scripting, you see yourself as you want to be and create a scenario in which you can play out this role again and again in your mind, until you have developed the assurance that you can do it. At the same time, you create an image reinforcer, such as a color, animal image, or expert, to remind yourself when in a real-life setting that you can do it just as you imagined in your mind.

In setting the scene for your scenario, use the setting where you want to use your new role. For example, if you want to develop a more assertive, authoritative personality to take over a managerial position in your company, picture yourself being more assertive and authoritative in your present position and see others responding to your new image in the appropriate way, such as listening to you more seriously and coming to you frequently for advice. At the same time, see yourself being authoritative and assertive in the position you want, and notice that people defer to you and respect you.

Likewise, if you want to be a warmer, friendlier person to get along better with co-workers, see yourself doing things in the office to express this warmth and friendliness—such as offering to make coffee for someone when you make some for yourself or greeting people with a big smile and a friendly comment.

You should use your usual relaxed, meditative state to picture or think about this scenario. At the same time, visualize or think of your image reinforcer in order to make an association between (1) the role you want to adopt, (2) the way you want to change to suit that role, and (3) the reminder to help you make that change.

Use the image reinforcer that feels most comfortable for you. The three types of images suggested here are (1) a color image, (2) animal image, and (3) expert image. The basic process is the same; what differs is the particular image you use as a reminder to act as you wish according to your mental script.

The Color Image Approach

In the color image approach, you image a color around your body representing the quality you would like to develop. For example, to be more aggressive, outgoing, dynamic, or assertive, picture an aggressive color, such as red. To be warmer and friendlier, picture a warm color, such as orange. To be more detail oriented and organized, use a color associated with intellectual ability, such as yellow. To be more articulate, use a color representing clarity, such as blue.

Each color is linked to certain common associations, and you may be likely to share them. But, whether you do or not, choose your color reinforcer based on your own color associations with that quality.

Later, when you are in a real situation and need additional support for your new trait, imagine this color is around you again, and let it infuse you with energy and confidence and help you play out your new role.

The Animal Imagery Technique

In the animal imagery technique, you visualize an animal representing the characteristic you want to acquire. Choose the animal based on your own associations with that animal, although there are certain common associations, as in the color approach. For example, to be warm and friendly, visualize a soft, furry animal, like a kitten or a puppy.

To be aggressive, visualize an active, aggressive animal like a wolf or fox. To be more articulate, visualize a talkative animal, like a dolphin or parrot.

Later, in the actual situation when you need a reinforcer, call up this animal image, so you will feel more confident to act as you wish.

The Expert Image Method

In the expert image method, you imagine yourself as an expert who is supremely skilled in the desired characteristics. Furthermore, you see yourself doing the kinds of things experts commonly do, such as talking about a new book on a TV talk show or giving a newspaper interview.

Later, in a real situation, you can draw on this image as a reminder of how you want to be.

USING THE IMAGE REINFORCER TECHNIQUES TO ACQUIRE SPECIFIC PERSONALITY TRAITS

The following examples illustrate how to use these image techniques with a scenario to develop a particular trait. These examples are based on some common qualities people seek to acquire for more success in a work situation. To acquire another trait, develop your own scenario around that, and feel free to use any reinforcer with any trait.

USE COLOR IMAGERY TO BECOME MORE
OUTGOING AND DYNAMIC   Time: 5-10 minutes

Start by imagining yourself in a situation in which you are more the way you want to be—in this case, outgoing and dynamic. Some possibilities include teaching a class or making a sale. See yourself in that situation and mentally play out that role as vividly as you can. Conclude by seeing the color you associate with those qualities, such as red, around you. The following example uses a business networking meeting. As usual, first close your eyes and relax.

See yourself arriving at the business networking event. You open the door and the event is in full swing. The atmosphere feels charged and full of energy, as people move around meeting and greeting each other. People are talking enthusiastically, clinking glasses, laughing, smiling. Some are exchanging business cards with one another or shaking hands.

You notice some people near the center of the room who look interesting. As you approach, you see they are wearing name tags that indicate they are in a profession you find of special interest to you.

Without hesitation, you go over to them, smile broadly, and say hello. Then, you make a comment that draws you instantly into the conversation, such as stating you were looking to meet someone in their field or just heard them mention a common associate. Whatever it is, you speak with confidence, so the others eagerly listen and respond. They find your business especially interesting, and they are open to the possibility of doing business with you. You conclude the conversation by exchanging business cards and saying you will be in touch later.

Then, you politely excuse yourself to move on to the next individual or group. When you do, you feel the same sense of assurance and know exactly what to say.

Spend about five minutes going from group to group in your mind. Then, before you leave, stand in the doorway for a moment. As you do, you see a color representing the personality qualities you have displayed—being outgoing and dynamic. This color may be red, or maybe some other color. It seems to surround you and radiates from you brightly.

Experience the strong energy or force radiating from this color for a few moments. This color will remain with you, and whenever you want to be more outgoing and dynamic, think of this color. It will appear around you again and give you a renewed charge of energy and self-confidence, so you can express these desired traits.

When you are ready, leave the business networking gathering and open your eyes.

Similarly, if you are in any other situation where you want to develop any personality trait using the color imagery approach, see yourself in this situation and vividly play out the role. (For instance, as a teacher, give a lecture in your mind; as a sales person, go over your presentation on a sales call.) Then, end your visualization by seeing the color around you. In the actual situation, visualize that color around yourself, too.

USE ANIMAL IMAGERY TO BECOME MORE WARM AND FRIENDLY   Time: 5-10 minutes

In the animal imagery approach, you first see yourself as an animal representing the qualities you want to develop, such as being warmer and friendlier to others. Then, with this image in mind, imagine yourself in a situation in which you want to express those qualities. Later the image will help you do this in real life, for you will act from the feelings associated with that image.

This scenario illustrates how this process might work if you want to improve your relationships with others by becoming more warm and friendly with your co-workers. Begin by closing your eyes and getting relaxed as usual.

See yourself as a soft, gentle, friendly animal, like a kitten or puppy. Someone is holding you in his lap and is stroking you. His strokes feel warm and comforting, and you feel cozy, protected. You feel very friendly and show this by alternately stretching and snuggling up in a small, cuddly ball. This person continues to stroke you, and you feel very peaceful, trusting, and content.

Now, with this image in mind, see yourself in a situation in which you want to be open and friendly with someone, such as in your office. Go up to that person and say something in a friendly, chatty way, certain they will respond in kind. They do, and you talk comfortably for several minutes, all conflicts from the past put aside, so you can work together more productively in the future.

Now, for a few minutes, hold these two images in mind, and alternately focus on the soft friendly animal and on the situation you have imagined. Later, when you are in a real situation where you want to be more open and friendly, think of the animal image, and it will help you attain this desired state.

You can use other animal imagery to reinforce other ways of acting. For instance, if you are going to an especially tough negotiation session, a wolf image might make you tougher. If you have to think through a difficult intellectual challenge, a wily fox image might help make you more mentally agile. If your job takes you into a dangerous neighborhood, perhaps a bear or lion image might give you added confidence.

Whatever the situation, focus on the animal image briefly, then visualize the situation you want to affect. Finally, in the real-life situation, recall that animal image to reinforce the way you want to act.

USE EXPERT IMAGERY TO BECOME
MORE ARTICULATE   Time: 5-10 minutes

The expert imagery method is especially apt when you need to feel powerful or be an authority on something. You start off by seeing yourself as an expert in a controlled situation, like a TV talk show or interview.

Then, if you have a situation in which you want to apply this feeling of power or expertise, you see yourself in that situation being effective and in charge. If you have no particular situation in mind and simply want to acquire an air of authority and expertise, omit this step.

The last phase of this exercise is applying this image in everyday life. You recall your image of you as the expert as a reminder that you can talk knowledgeably and confidently about the subject at hand.

To begin, close your eyes and relax. Now see yourself as an expert on some subject. You have just written a book about it and are a guest on a TV talk show. You feel calm, comfortable. You know your subject matter perfectly and are ready to answer any questions.

The cameras start rolling and your host begins the interview. How did you come to write your book? Where did you get your material? Why do you feel your book has been successful? What do you think of such and such? What advice would you give others? And so on. As you answer each question, your host listens attentively and seems impressed by your wide knowledge of your field.

Keep on talking and answering questions for several minutes. Be aware of how good it feels to be so knowledgeable and to express what you think and feel.

Now, if there is some situation in life in which you want to be regarded as an expert or authority, see yourself in that situation. You have just left a very successful national tour as an expert, and you bring that expertise and assurance to this situation. For example, you may be giving a presentation, making an important sales call, trying to convince someone to hire or give you a promotion. Whatever the situation, see yourself responding knowledgeably and confidently, just as you did on the TV talk show.

Later, in a real life situation, recall this image of you, the expert, and know that you are able to talk knowledgeably and with complete assurance about your topic.

 *Chapter 10*

How to Better Understand and Improve Your Relationships with Others

By understanding others better, you can improve your ability to relate to them and up your chances for success, too. For example, in a job interview, the more you know about how your interviewer thinks, the better you can present yourself. In a business deal, you can use your insight to determine if a prospective associate is someone you can trust and work with effectively. If you are selling a product, you can sense the kind of message your prospect would most like to hear and tailor your presentation accordingly. The advantages are endless.

Debbie C. Avoided Unscrupulous People with Mind Power

Debbie C., for example, used her inner knowing to steer clear of several partnerships that could have been a disaster. Previously, as an artist and designer, she had gotten into a number of arrangements with business   103 people, who had taken advantage of her lack of business acumen, and she had unwisely trusted their claims about what they could do. But then, it turned out that these people didn't have the skills or contacts they said. One man turned out to be an alcoholic, and his promises to set Debbie up in a design studio were pure chimera, because he was more interested in a romance with her than a business arrangement. A financeer talked gradiosely about the financing he could arrange to get Debbie's cards and posters on the market. But then, the day before the money from some doctor friends was supposed to come through, the financeer discovered that his business partner had been embezzling from the company, and he put all other business deals on hold. And Debbie had several other aborted business arrangements.

However, in a workshop, Debbie discovered how to use mind power techniques to get valid insights into people, and suddenly she was able to steer clear of the business flakes who make empty promises and discover the people who were genuine and sincere.

For instance, in one case, she met a promoter who wanted to start a travel club. He talked about how he wanted her to join the staff to design all of the club's materials and take charge of the decor for the clubroom and club plane. She would get an excellent salary; be part of the club's executive board; have travel privileges; get shares of stock in the company; and enjoy many other benefits. He talked convincingly, and Debbie was about to do some preliminary work for him on speculation, while he was, he claimed, waiting for the funds from a stock issue to come through.

But as they talked, Debbie's inner radar began picking up some danger signals. She couldn't explain it. But she experienced a knotted up feeling in her stomach and saw the image of a black raven warning her to watch out as he spoke. As a result, she calmly told the man she would have to think about his proposal and asked him to leave his business plan. When she did some checking, she learned he was operating his business out of his bedroom; that he only had promises of backing; and that there was no stock issue. Also, she discovered that several other people who had worked for him on speculation had ended up with nothing.

Similarly, Debbie used her inner powers a few weeks later when an associate introduced her to a man who showed off an impressive résumé with a list of video and film credits. Now he had some ideas for dolls and bean bags he wanted her to design. As he explained the project, he talked expansively about the many worthy social projects he wanted to finance with the money from these items, such as transforming the education of children and adults.

Yet, as they spoke, Debbie heard her inner voice repeating the warning: "Beware...Beware. This man isn't what he seems." As with the travel promoter, she couldn't put her finger on anything special that made her feel this way, as, outwardly, everything the man said seemed reasonable. For instance, he bragged a great deal about all he could do and dropped many names of the people he knew; yet while she found this bragging annoying, she had met other people who were equally egotistical, although some were extremely successful. Likewise, the man's casual dress for their business meeting, while unusual, wasn't necessarily an unfavorable sign; nor was the somewhat run-down apartment house where he lived—she had met other people who were struggling on their way up to achieve ultimate success. Even the man's pushiness, while offensive to her, could be an advantage if he was going to be selling her products.

But for whatever reason, the message came through to her loud and clear—don't work with this man, you'll only have problems. Thus, she diplomatically talked of being busy with many projects; and later her intuitions were confirmed, when she heard from others who had dealings with this person. They reported he was difficult to work with, unrealistic in his expectations, unfamiliar with trade practices in the industry he wanted to enter, and unwilling to listen to reasonable suggestions. Instead, they said, he tended to blow up, accuse others of not being smart enough to see things his way, and threaten to get someone else to do what he wanted.

Thus, by being in touch with her inner powers and trusting them to pick up insights about people, Debbie was able to avoid some problem situations.

"GUT" FEELINGS LED TO WISE DECISIONS

Conversely, I have used my inner knowing to make some quick decisions about people which have led to good long-term financial and business arrangements. For example, for the last six years, I have made almost instant assessments of people who wanted to rent some space in my house. True, most people rely on references, and some spend extensive time checking credit background and calling previous landlords. But I have found it works for me to ask a few questions, get an overall impression of the person, and listen to my inner feelings to get a yes or no. In every case—involving ten people over a six-year period—things have worked out. I have sensed that the people I selected to move in with me would be quiet, responsible, stable, neat, considerate people—the qualities I look for in a housemate—and that's exactly what they turned out to be.

Another associate, Paul G., who has a business distributing specialty health and food products, uses these techniques to custom tailor his sales presentations and increase his chances of closing a deal. He has dozens of products he can show people and a list of over twenty benefits his products offer. But he selects only a few products and benefits to emphasize depending on the insights he gets about a person.

He starts getting these intuitions with his first phone call. As he asks a few preliminary screening questions to determine if the person would be a good customer, he forms an image of this person in his mind and gradually creates a total picture. This picture may differ from the person's actual physical appearance, but it gives Paul an intuitive sense of the person's personality, character, and preferred way of perceiving and receiving information.

Then, when he meets the person, Paul uses this preliminary picture to shape his opening remarks, and as they talk further, he continues to refine this image to better know this person. The result has been that Paul has excellent rapport with his prospects; in essence, he senses where the other person is at and relates to him or her from that person's own perspective. Then, after spending a few minutes to cement this rapport, Paul draws on his mental picture of the person to emphasize those features of his products and business he thinks will have the most appeal.

These efforts, in turn, show up in his sales. In a year, Paul has created a thriving specialty business, with several thousand dollars each month in personal retail sales, and a sales organization of several dozen other distributors whom Paul motivates with these methods, too.

THE TYPE OF INFORMATION GAINED THROUGH MIND-POWER TECHNIQUES

These mind power techniques provide us insights into others, because they enable us to tune into the other person's inner essence or self. Essentially, the process is much like getting a gut level feeling about someone and using that to decide whether to trust him or not. However, by working with your inner powers, you are learning to refine these intuitive feelings, so you can use them to gain more precise information.

You might compare the process to first seeing normally and then looking through a magnifying glass, so you see whatever you want to learn about more clearly and larger than life.

Your inner abilities can be developed to work that way. First, you can train yourself to become more sensitive to ordinary outer cues, such as clothing, gestures, and facial expressions, because we learn much about a person's real character through his or her outward appearances and behaviors. For instance, a woman who wears a lot of bright colors to work is probably a more outgoing, friendly, dramatic person than someone who wears blues and browns or soft pastels.

Then you can go even deeper to discover what a person is really like inside. You can find out about his or her character, sense of integrity, perspective, and preferred way of receiving information and communicating with you. Your mind powers can help you learn about someone in three ways:

1. to get a quick first impression when you meet someone new;
2. to get an advance impression when you set up a meeting with someone, so you can have a better first meeting; and
3. to gain a more in-depth understanding of a person, so you can communicate and interact better or give that person useful advice.

BECOMING AWARE OF PERSONALITY TYPES AND BEHAVIORAL STYLES

Your mind powers can give you these insights, because they make you more aware of the person's inner personality type and behavioral style. Then you can use this information to make any interaction go more smoothly or decide if you want to interact, continue an interaction, or interact more closely with a person.

This information about a person helps us make interaction decisions, as each personality type is characterized by certain traits, ways of viewing the world, and preferences in relating to others. Then, too, every person, whatever his or her personal style, has a dimension of personality based on a sense of ethics and integrity. Although all of us have a mixture of traits comprising our personalities, our types or behavioral styles refer to our primary orientations to the world and others.

There are a number of terms used to characterize people according to personality type in different systems. For example, the DISC theory, which is growing in popularity in the business community and is used by some management trainers, derives from the work of William Marsten, who researched the emotions of normal people. He developed a four-dimensional model based on the notion that each person has four basic drives in different combinations, and he characterized these four primary types (D) high in dominance and directness (I) high in influence and interest in people, (S) high in steadiness and stability, and (C) high in conscientiousness and competence. The psychologist Carl Jung divides people up into those who are combinations of thinking and feeling or knowing and sensing. Other groups use other terms.

I prefer to combine the concepts from these different approaches and use the action-oriented terms below, which characterize people according to their primary perceptual and behavior style: (1) The Take-Charge Personality, (2) The Analyzer/Explorer, (3) The People Person, and (4) The Conscientious Planner. The take-charge person tends to have a strongly developed ability to take in information by hearing it; the analyzer/explorer has a well-developed visual sense; the people person tends to experience sensations and respond emotionally or expressively; and the conscientious planner often has a feeling of knowing or certainty about how things are or will be. Each person of course, may be a mixture of these different types.

Use whatever terminology for these personality types with which you feel most comfortable. The important point is to recognize that people have different perceptual and behavioral styles, and to most effectively relate to them, you should be aware of their perspective, as people are most responsive to someone who relates to them in terms of their own point of view. Thus, an employer using this awareness can manage his or her employees better; an employee can make things go more smoothly with his or her boss; a salesperson can be more likely to have a receptive customer and close a sale.

Chart 6 illustrates the major characteristics of people with the four different personality types. Also, it indicates the way these people prefer to interact with others. As you pick up information about people using your mind powers, you will improve your abilities to interact with them (or decide not to interact with them) by keeping these characteristics and preferences in mind.

Chart 7 describes the major types of ethical styles based on a person's morality and sense of integrity. This will help you decide how far you want to trust the person with whom you are interacting, whatever his or her personality type.

CHART #6

Personality Types and Personal Characteristics

Personality Type	Major Characteristics	Preferred Types of Response
The Take-Charge Personality	Assertive, aggressive, direct, energetic, organized. Interested in broad overviews, trends. A leader type.	Likes someone to be direct, to the point. Likes someone to get behind his or her ideas, plans, and support them.
The Analyzer/Explorer	Cool, calm, detached, independent. Curious, an explorer. Concerned with seeing how things fit together. An evaluator/ analyzer type.	Likes someone to be clear, organized, provide a full picture. Likes someone with an analytical mind.
The People Person	Sensitive, emotional, dependent on others. Concerned with details. Very aware of and responsive to people. Concerned with making things go smoothly. Often a follower or helper type.	Likes someone to provide details. Likes someone to be warm, feeling, responsive.
The Conscientious Planner	Very perceptive, quick to know something. Often critical, judgmental, or feels he or she knows it all. Frequently opinionated, righteous. A good sense of what will happen, how things will turn out. A planner, organizer type.	Likes someone to be agreeable, receptive to his or her ideas. Likes someone to be organized, self-assured, and confident.

CHART #7

ETHICAL STYLES

Ethical Style	Major Characteristics	Considerations When Interacting
The Complete Moralist	Completely honest and expects total honesty and integrity from others. May sometimes be very righteous or have a strong religious base for this morality.	Expect to be very honest and straight with this person. Feel confident that you can trust this person completely.
The Situational Moralist	Adapts his or her ethical response to the situation or person. If others in the situation are behaving morally and ethically, he or she will, too.	Be very honest and straight with this person, and he or she will be honest and straight with you. Also, make sure this person is aware you are doing this, for if this person has any reason to distrust you, you may find he or she is no longer being straight with you, but instead is acting like a pragmatic moralist.
The Pragmatic Moralist	Totally amoral. Acts honestly and ethically when it is to his or her advantage to do so. But can engage in dishonest or unethical activities at any moment, if it seems profitable to do so, and there is a low risk of getting caught.	Be wary in any dealings with this individual. As long as he or she thinks there is some personal gain in it, he or she will be straight with you. But if you lose your value, this person will have no qualms about acting unethically toward you.

APPLYING THE MIND POWER TECHNIQUES TO GAIN INSIGHTS AND INFORMATION

Keep these personality, behavioral, and ethical styles in mind as you use your mind power abilities to get insights and information about others. The following techniques illustrate how you can apply your mind powers to achieve these ends.

1. Get a Quick First Impression When You Meet Someone

You can get a quick insight into someone when you first meet them for whatever reason—as a potential customer, client, employer, employee, business partner—in two key ways:

- through your most immediate auditory or visual impressions when you first approach the person;
- through your first impressions when you physically touch the person with a handshake or hug.

In both cases, you gain this insight by listening to your inner voice or by noticing any spontaneous images that appear when you meet. This will give you cues about the person. For example, suppose that when you are introduced to a new business associate, you hear your inner voice say the word "tiger"; or suppose you see a tiger image briefly flash before you in your mind's eye. Those brief insights are significant, for they suggest that the person might have the characteristics you associate with a tiger, such as being wily, aggressive, and tenacious. Then, in dealing with this person, you can take these qualities into account.

The following exercises will help you become more aware of your first impressions and will give you feedback on your accuracy, so you can feel more confident of your abilities. You will find your sensitivity to others will increase as you practice paying more attention to your initial responses.

In doing these exercises, carry a small pad or notebook with you to jot down your impressions when you first observe or meet someone. You should make these notes discreetly. For example, if you're in a class or meeting situation, where you can take notes on the spot, fine. If not, find a place where you can make your notes unobserved as soon as possible after your observations.

When you get to know the person better or learn about him or her from others, compare your initial impressions with what you learn later. You'll find you are quite accurate and that your accuracy increases with practice. There are three types of initial impressions to observe: (1) when you first see someone; (2) when you first meet someone; and (3) when you make an initial physical contact by shaking hands. The following exercises illustrate how to do this.

FIRST IMPRESSIONS   Time: 1-3 minutes

Get Impressions When You First See Someone. *This technique is ideal for when you go to an event and see someone you expect to talk to or meet later. Or use it at a meeting when you first arrive and no one has said anything yet. Look at each person you want to know about in turn, and think of the first word or picture that comes to mind. Write down as soon as you can and think what that word or image means to you. That will give you a general impression of the person. After you meet the person, review your comments to see how accurate you were—and watch your accuracy increase as you continue to do this.*

Get Impressions When You First Meet Someone. *This technique is ideal for almost any sort of gathering where you can meet someone yourself or can observe that person meeting and talking with others. As you walk up to and meet the person yourself, be aware of any words or images that pop up when the person speaks to a group or meets another person. Then, write down these words and images as soon as you can and think about what they mean. Later, as you get to know this person or see him or her in action, review your comments to check your level of accuracy.*

Get Impressions When You Make an Initial Physical Contact by Shaking Hands. *Whenever you shake hands with someone you meet and expect to engage in further conversation, you can use this technique for getting impressions and checking your accuracy. While you shake hands, focus your awareness on that handshake, and notice any words or images that appear in your mind's eye at this time. Ask yourself what they mean to you, and then, if you continue to converse, check your accuracy. How much did this first impression tell you about the person? And how consistent is this impression with what you sense or learn from the person as you talk? Again, you'll find your accuracy goes up with practice.*

---

2. Get Advance Impressions of Someone Before You Meet

When you are about to meet someone you don't know, whether for a job interview, a potential business deal, or whatever, some advance insight about this person's personality type can help you act so the meeting goes more smoothly.

The personality types and behavioral styles described earlier will give you the framework in which to organize the insights you receive. It is also helpful to gather together and review any preliminary information you have about the person, including name, nickname, occupational title, photograph, organizations the person belongs to, and the like.

Once you have this information in mind, you are ready to perform this technique.

ADVANCE IMPRESSIONS   Time: 3-5 minutes

Get relaxed, close your eyes, and call up an image or the name of the person you are going to meet in your mind's eye. Concentrate on making this image or name expand and contract for about one minute. Then, see the image form into a white ball of energy, and watch that energy swirl around for another minute and form into a computer screen. Then, on that screen, a word appears that describes a person as a take-charge personality, an analyzer/explorer, a people person, or a conscientious planner. Should two or more names appear simultaneously, you know the person is a combination of these primary types.

Then, with that word and its associated traits in mind, see yourself meeting this person for the first time. As you do, notice what you say and how you act. Later, when you meet the person, this mental rehearsal will help you make a good impression and relate to the person from his or her perspective.

---

3. Get In-depth Insight into Others

After you have met someone and have initiated an ongoing relationship, these in-depth techniques can help you gain additional insights about the person or further your relationship. In a work or business setting, these methods can be particularly useful in promoting smoother relationships with co-workers, managing a work team more effectively, or influencing an employer to regard you more favorably.

These techniques work by focusing your intuitive abilities on reading the individual's personality in more depth than an initial impression. As such, they are much like the techniques used by professionals who do a personality reading on someone in the course of spiritual or psychic counseling. These professionals may be quite accurate as they know special techniques and have practiced extensively. But everyone has these intuitive abilities. The more you practice with them, the more accurate and detailed information you will get.

The basic approach is to use an object, imagery, or new way of seeing to perceive information about someone. You gain this information intuitively from calling up images of the person's past, body, thoughts, or surrounding energy field. The person can be physically present or not. If he or she isn't present, just visualize him or her in front of you.

You can use the following images or create your own symbol systems. Any imagery system will work if you get used to it.

To become more accurate, try reading some people you don't know well; then ask for feedback to check your accuracy. If you're off at first, don't worry. Your accuracy will improve with practice, along with your confidence.

To begin, get relaxed for all of these techniques, and except for the aura technique, close your eyes. Preferably, sit upright in a receptive position.

PSYCHOMETRY. (USING AN OBJECT TO LEARN ABOUT OTHERS)
Time: 5-10 minutes

To begin, ask someone for a small object. Then, hold it in your hand and meditate on it. See it in your mind's eye. Try touching it to your forehead. Notice what words, images, or impressions appear. Say them aloud if the person is present. Write them down if you like. These impressions can provide clues to the person's personality, interests, relationships, life style, and so forth. After you share your impressions with your subject, get some feedback.

READING A PERSON'S ENERGY CENTERS
Time: 5-10 minutes

According to many holistic health and spiritual traditions, each person has a series of energy concentrations or centers in the body, located from the base of the spine to the top of the head. These centers, sometimes called "chakras" (a term borrowed from the Hindus and Buddhists), can provide a window into a person's inner self, because his or her personality is reflected by the flow of energy through the body.

There are seven primary centers, each linked with a different personal quality. These are:

1. the base of the spine—survival
2. the reproductive area—sexual energy
3. the stomach or solar plexus—identity, will
4. the heart—warmth and emotions
5. the throat—communication
6. the center of the forehead (third eye)—perception
7. the top of the head (crown chakra)—spirituality

To read someone's energy centers, sit in front of him or her or visualize him or her before you. Then, after you relax and close your eyes, visualize as follows:

In this process, you'll imagine a rose in front of each energy center in turn. But first, see the petals alone or the whole rose and stem by itself.

Now start at the base of the spine. Place an image of the rose in front of this energy center, and observe what happens to the rose. Does it change color or shape? Begin to move? Assume the shape of an animal or person? Does anything else happen to it? Let the impressions come spontaneously, and don't try to analyze. Say them aloud or write them down, as you wish.

Then, once these images stop coming, ask yourself what they mean to you in light of the characteristics associated with this energy center. Notice what impressions or explanations spontaneously come, and jot them down.

Now go on to the next energy center and observe what happens to the rose again and ask what this means. Keep doing this until you conclude with the energy center at the top of the head.

In performing this exercise, be aware that there is no fixed meaning for any image. It depends on what the images or symbols mean to you, as every person is different and has a different symbol system. Also, an image means different things depending on which energy center it is associated with. For example, if a rose appears to open up and become very bright in front of the first energy center (associated with survival), this suggests the person may be very ambitious, because he or she is acting strongly in the area of survival. But if the same image appears in front of the heart center, it may suggest the person is very warm and emotional, as his or her heart is opening up.

LEARNING ABOUT A PERSON'S PAST OR FUTURE   Time: 5-15 minutes

You can read someone's present and past whether he or she is with you or not. You simply see this person before you in your mind's eye, if he or she is not there. In either case, use the following scenario as a guide.

Now, on your mental screen, see yourself going into a large library.

A large marble stairway is before you. You go up the stairs, and at the top you see a door with a sign that says, "Reference." You go in and enter a large room, with many long tables and files. You walk toward a series of large file drawers in the center of the room. There are some letters on each file, and you look for the drawer with the letter corresponding to the name of your subject. When you find it, pull out this drawer and flip through the cards.

Finally, you come to that person's name and pull out his or her card. There is a date on the top right hand corner. Look at it. It designates a period in this person's life. Or it may refer to a past or future lifetime. To learn what happened (or will happen), look at the center of the card. A biography is written there. Read it and learn what you want to know.

After you read it, put the card back. If you wish, pull out another card and read it, too. Then, when you are ready, leave the library. Go down the same marble stairs, and when you return to the street, return to normal consciousness.

As a variation on this technique, enter the library with a time period in mind and find a card with that date. Visualize the cards arranged in a time sequence, and flip through the cards until you find the right date.

After you complete the reading, it helps to record your impressions so you can better remember them. Later, get feedback when you can to test your perception. If you can't ask your subject directly (for instance, you might not feel comfortable telling your boss, "I've been trying to learn about you intuitively"), see if you can bring up the topic in the course of conversation. You'll find your accuracy improves over time, and even if some specific details are wrong, you'll find your overall impression is correct. (For instance, you get an image of your business partner as a boxing champ as a teenager, whereas he was in fights to protect himself from some gangs in the neighborhood.)

You can use these insights to help you build a better relationship with this person today. For instance, some of these insights might suggest topics of conversation to improve your rapport (if you sense the person has been a scrappy fighter since childhood, perhaps comment on a recent newspaper article about someone who has bested some toughs and foiled a crime). Perhaps these insights might give you some guidance in how to relate. Say you get an image of the person as an ardent explorer. That might suggest giving the person additional challenges to solve if you are that person's employer; or perhaps you might suggest some new ventures or company projects, if that person is a business partner or boss.

UNDERSTANDING SOMEONE THROUGH IDENTIFICATION

Time: 5-10 minutes

Another way to gain information about someone to improve your relationship is using your mind power abilities to identify closely with that person. One approach is illustrated in the following exercise in which you imagine yourself putting on another person's head and responding as he or she would. Use the following guide to experience this.

To begin, close your eyes and get relaxed. Now visualize this person standing in front of you. Observe his or her face carefully. Notice his or her eyes, lips, and bone structure. Look at how he or she smiles.

Next, stretch out your arms and lift his head from his body and place it on yours. Now look around and experience how the world looks through his eyes. What do you see? Hear? Feel? Now ask yourself questions about your new self—whatever you want to know. Ask them as "I" questions—What do I like to do? Where did I live as a child? What kind of work do I do? Don't try to answer consciously—just let the answers pop into your mind. Then, say your answers aloud or write them down.

After you finish your questions, take the head off and put it back on the person's body. Then, return to normal consciousness and open your eyes.

Later, if you can, get feedback (either directly or in the course of ordinary conversation) from this person to check your accuracy. With practice, your ability will improve.

TAKE A VISUAL VISIT

Time: 5-10 minutes

Another way to gain information, as you develop your intuitive powers, is to project your consciousness outside your body and imagine visiting a person's house. The way the house looks in your imagination, whether accurate or not, will tell you something about who that person is.

To begin, visualize the person you want to visit. It can be someone you know or not. Then, see yourself leaving your body in a rush of energy, which rises up from the base of your spine, spirals up, and goes out through your head. Then this energy continues to rise, lifting your inner self with it, until you come up a soft, white cloud floating by. You get off here, and for a few minutes, you float, feeling completely peaceful, calm, and free.

Now it is time to descend for your visit. Float down off your cloud, and below you, see this person's house. Note what it looks like. Observe the surroundings. Then, float in through the door. If anyone is there, do not talk to him. Just observe. What is the interior like? How many rooms? How large? What shape? How about the furnishings? Are there any animals or plants? Who else lives here besides this person? Then ask yourself what each of these images tells you about this person.

When you are finished, return to your cloud and float back to where you first got off. Then, spiral down, and let your energy and consciousness return to your head.

After your experience, record any details, and later, if possible, get feedback from the person you visited to check your accuracy. How accurately did you perceive his or her house? More importantly, how accurate were you in describing the characteristics of this person from your observations?

HOW TO READ AURAS TO OBTAIN MORE INFORMATION ABOUT PEOPLE

You can visualize an electro magneticenergy field around every person. Some research has suggested this is a real physical field, because Kirlian photography has been used to photograph the radiant heat surrounding the physical body. If you prefer, just think of a radiating energy capsule surrounding the body. It is often called the aura.

Depending on a person's state of mind, mood, and personality, and your perceptions of the person, you will see this field expand, contract, or change color. By training yourself to see in a new way, you can see or sense this aura, and obtain information about the person from it. This technique explains how.

UNDERSTANDING THE AURA

First, here are a few general characteristics about auras, so you will understand what you see. An aura will usually look like a light filmy after-image surrounding each person. It tends to expand when a person is positive, healthy, active, assertive, or thinks of power; and to contract when one is negative, ill, passive, withdrawn, or thinks of weakness. It frequently will appear with colors—usually light, fuzzy, pastel tones—and these colors express a person's personality traits. However, one observer may perceive these differently than another, as each person is different, and the observer-subject interaction differs in each case. However, certain color associations are common. These are:

- Red—energy, power, courage, strength, love, warmth
- Yellow—intellect, thought
- Orange—sexuality, activity, joy
- Green—health, healing, spiritual growth

- Blue—peace, calm, spirituality, coolness
- Purple—royalty, mysticism, spiritual truth
- White—purity, spiritual attainment
- Gray, Black—sadness, depression, illness

Now, let's work on observing the aura.

OBSERVING THE AURA   Time: 5-10 minutes

To see the aura, look at the person in an unfocused way, as if staring off in the distance. Then, keep looking. The aura will emerge as a frame of light and color around the person. Usually it will appear around his or her head first, as a white shimmer of energy, and then it may encircle the whole body as well. At first, you may see only white. But as you practice, colors should appear. These will have a fuzzy, pastel quality.

In time, you can see auras under any condition. Just look, and they will appear. However, to facilitate seeing them initially, practice under optimal conditions—in a quiet place, with dim lighting. Ideally, have your subject (perhaps a friend you are practicing with) sit against a large white or softly colored wall. Then, stare at the center of his or her forehead for a few minutes. Watch for a fuzzy whiteness to appear around the head. This is the aura. Gradually it may grow larger and brighter. It may vary in size and intensity around different parts of the body. Soft colors may emerge. Later you can interpret their meaning.

Once the aura emerges, you can shift your eyes to observe the aura around different parts of the body. But keep your awareness unfocused. Should the aura begin to fade. look back at the subject's forehead, until you see the aura's strength return.

After several minutes of looking, share your observations with your subject, and interpret the colors you have seen. Again, seek feedback about your accuracy, and use this to help you improve.

Two Aura Exercises

To further develop your ability to see auras, here are some aura exercises you can try with a friend. One of you should meditate on some idea or image to affect your aura, while the other observes. Then, the observer compares his or her perceptions with what the meditator was doing. You'll be amazed at your accuracy. Two experiments to try are:

1. One person concentrates on the imagery of power or weakness to expand or contract the aura, while the other observes.

2. One person concentrates on sending his or her energy to the left or right, while the other observes.

How to Apply Insights Gained from the Aura

Once you are sensitive to perceiving the aura and understanding what this tells you about the person, you can apply this information on an ongoing basis to build a better relationship. This can be especially useful in a business setting for building rapport with the individuals you work with or for relating to clients and customers.

For example, reading a person's aura can make you more sensitive to everyday mood swings, so you can react appropriately. For instance, say you approach your boss to ask for a raise and you notice a great deal of red and gray in his aura, suggesting a mixture of anger and sadness, although outwardly he looks calm and impassive as usual. This insight tells you this may not be the best time to make such a request; rather you will probably do better if you wait for a time when you sense that his aura has more positive colors, such as red combined with yellow, orange, or green, suggesting power, warmth, happiness, and health.

Similarly, if you are in a negotiation session with someone, you might pick up information about the person's relative strength or willingness to give in or compromise from the aura. For instance, if you see lots of reds in the aura, that suggests the person is feeling strong and powerful, and you'll have to strengthen your own position to prevail. But if you begin to see yellows, this suggests the person is becoming more thoughtful and is perhaps ready to compromise. Should you see blues or dark colors, perhaps the person is ready to concede and it's time to press towards a close.

In short, you can use information from an aura reading to supplement the other more visible cues a person is giving off in the form of body language, gestures, facial cues, words, and eye movements.

APPLYING THE MIND POWER TECHNIQUES TO IMPROVE YOUR RELATIONSHIPS

Beside gaining insights and information, you can use your mind power abilities to directly affect your relationships. The most usual way is to make people feel better about the relationship by chasing away any negative, angry feelings or by emphasizing warm, supportive, friendly, loving feelings. Sometimes, too, people use these techniques to reinforce their own feelings of power in a relationship and make others more aware they have this power.

The basic process involves focusing your mental energy on another person as you visualize your goal in the relationship and mentally sending a message about this to the person. This process works on two levels. First, it helps you change your own attitude toward the person, so when you see each other again, you will interact in terms of your desired goal, which will influence the other person to respond accordingly. Secondly, as thoughts have energy, the person to whom you direct this thought transmission will receive it on an inner psychic or mental level. Consciously, he or she may not be aware of your message. But your mental communication may inspire or remind him or her to relate to you in this desired way.

One common use of this approach is smoothing the way for a future meeting with someone. Also, some people use this method to send their thoughts to encourage someone to get in touch with them. The following exercises will help you use mind power techniques to improve relationships in various ways.

Creating a Warmer Relationship

To overcome angry feelings, resentments, misunderstandings, or generally make someone feel warm, friendly, and positive toward you, sending love is the perfect antidote. It will help eliminate any negative feelings and make you feel good. Someone who seems distant will seem closer. If you and an associate have any angry feelings toward each other, your positive thoughts can turn the situation around; so when you see each other again, the conflict may be gone.

The first exercise involves sending love to prepare the way for a better meeting with someone. The second is designed to both send love and persuade someone to contact you.

SENDING LOVE   Time: 3-5 minutes

Put up a picture of the person to whom you're sending love before you and imagine a glowing ball of love radiating out from your heart. Direct a beam of love

from your heart to this person. As you do, say the word "love" over and over to yourself, and send these words along this beam. As this beam arrives, notice that the person begins to glow and radiates love back. Continue to focus on this image for several minutes. Notice how it becomes more and more brilliant as you continue sending love.

Now visualize the next meeting you expect to have with this person. See the setting as vividly as possible. Notice whatever is around you, imagine what the person is wearing, what he or she is doing, and so on. Then, as you approach, continue to feel these warm, friendly feelings, and notice that the other person responds the same way. If you have felt any anger or resentments towards each other, that is gone. After this initial meeting, continue your conversation, and notice that you have a good rapport. When you conclude the conversation, you feel fully satisfied that you have achieved your goal.

PROMOTING COMMUNICATION   Time: 3-5 minutes

To get someone to contact you or be more receptive to a call from you, you will visualize sending this person a message. However, if you feel there has been any problem in the relationship you must overcome first (such as an argument or feelings of resentment), or if you want to make the relationship warmer, start by sending love as in the previous exercise. Then, use the following mind to mind communication technique to promote the desired contact.

Take a few minutes about the same time each day to get relaxed in a quiet place. Then visualize the person you want to communicate with in your mind's eye. Now mentally ask him or her to contact you or be receptive to your call by imagining a cable of pure white energy radiating from your mind to this person with your message. Imagine that this beam of energy continues to transmit this request for about three minutes. Then, see this person contacting you by phone, by letter, or in person—however you wish to receive the message, or being receptive when you initiate contact.

Do this regularly for several days, and quite frequently, you'll find the person will call. Or if the person hasn't, feel confident you have paved the way for a successful call when you call yourself.

PROMOTING A CLOSER RELATIONSHIP   Time: 3-5 minutes

Another way to promote a closer relationship or get someone to contact you is by using an object representing you and the other person, such as a candle, to help you focus and reinforce your message. This technique has frequently been used when a love relationship is involved, but you can also use it to promote friendships and closer understandings with the people you work with. As in the previous exercise for Promoting Communication, take a few minutes each day for several days until your message starts having its effect. The following example uses candles for the object, but you can use whatever you feel most comfortable with, such as small figurines, statues, or even pens and pencils, to represent you and the other person.

To prepare, get two candles, one representing you and the other the person you want to hear from. (For example, pink and blue candles might be used for a woman and man respectively, although any colors with personal meaning are fine.) The first day you do this technique, set the candles about twelve inches apart. On each successive day when you begin, place the candles two inches closer together, until on the seventh day, they touch. Thereafter, leave the candles touching.

Now light the candles and turn off any lights. Look back and forth from one candle to another for about one minute. Then close your eyes and see the candles burning in your mind's eye. Next see the two flames draw together, until they become a single flame. Observe the bright yellow beam that radiates out of this flame.

Now put one hand around each candle and hold your hands there, while you visualize this beam traveling across space and time to the person you want to contact you. Continue to hold these candles and concentrate on this image for about three minutes. Then, gently, push each candle about an inch towards the other (or if they are already together, press them together tightly). As you do this, think to yourself: "We are drawing closer and closer together. We are drawing closer and closer together. May he (she) contact me. (Or be receptive to my call.)" Or express these sentiments in your own words. Then, when you feel the message has been sent, let go of the candles, return to normal consciousness, and open your eyes.

Leave the candles in position, if you plan to do this technique again. Do this exercise regularly for about a week, and expect your call. Quite frequently, the person will have called you by then. If not, feel confident your call will be successful and contact the person yourself.

INCREASING YOUR POWER IN A RELATIONSHIP

To increase your power balance in a relationship, use the same principle as in the previous techniques designed to create warmer feelings. Essentially, you do a visualization or mental scenario in which you experience yourself being powerful. Then, you imagine yourself in a scene with this person that is likely to happen, in which you express this newfelt sense of power.

The following exercise provides a sample scenario you can use to increase your feelings of power and change the relationship accordingly.

BECOMING MORE POWERFUL   Time: 3-5 minutes

Put up a picture of the person you want to experience your greater power, and see the image of something you consider powerful before you as well. For example, it might be a powerful animal like a lion, a powerful piece of machinery like a steel press, a powerful vehicle like a rocket ship, a powerful type of person like a weight lifter or body builder. Concentrate on seeing this image vividly before you and feel the power that radiates from this image.

Then, direct a beam of your energy from your power center in your stomach area to this object, animal, or person. See yourself enter this image and become it. As you do so, say the word "power" over and over to yourself, and send these words along this beam. Notice that you are becoming and feeling more and more powerful as you do, and notice that the person you want to impress is also aware of this. Continue to focus on this image for several moments, and notice how it becomes stronger and stronger as you continue to beam your power into this image.

Now visualize the next meeting you expect to have with this person. See the setting as vividly as possible. Notice whatever is around you. Imagine what the person is wearing and doing. Then, as you approach, continue to feel these strong, powerful feelings, and notice that the other person responds accordingly. For example, he or she regards you with increased respect, is more deferential, is more willing to listen to you, and so forth. Notice, too, that any feelings of uncertainty you may have felt are completely gone, and you feel completely confident and sure of yourself. Once you meet, continue your conversation, and continue to relate to this person from your power place. When you conclude the conversation, you feel fully satisfied that you have achieved your goal.

INFLUENCING YOUR RELATIONSHIPS IN OTHER WAYS

You'll find that using these mind power techniques will have a marked affect on your relationships, either by changing the way you relate or by modifying how others perceive and respond to you.

While many people are especially interested in improving the emotional tone or power balance in a relationship, you can also create your own techniques to influence your relationships in other ways. For instance, maybe you want to take more initiative or responsibility in the relationship, and you want the other person to give you more space or trust so you can do this (as might be the case when an employee wants to expand his job responsibilities). Then, devise a visualization based on an image of something that takes initiative or responsibility (such as a fox), direct your beam of energy into that, and see yourself interacting with the person in this way. Or maybe you want more freedom and independence (perhaps to set your own hours and schedule). Then, create an image of freedom of independence (such as a bird), beam yourself into that, and visualize an interaction with the person.

In short, make these exercises your own by using symbols with meaning for you, and you'll find your relationships change dramatically in the direction you want.

 *Chapter 11*

How to Use Mind Power to Solve Problems and Make Decisions Through Brainstorming

THE VALUE OF THE BRAINSTORMING PROCESS

Brainstorming can be a quick and easy way to cut through difficult problems and make decisions. For example, Arne S., a sales manager in a medium-sized company serving the computer industry had a problem in his office. Sales of computers and computer parts were declining, and company sales were accordingly spiraling down. He felt he had to let some people go, although he hated to do it, as his company had developed a spirit of closeness among its employees. So he found it extremely difficult to make the decision himself.

Instead, Arne came up with an alternative. He brought his staff members together, explained the problem, and asked them to brainstorm alternatives with which they would feel more comfortable. The group spent about an hour coming up with suggestions—have a lottery; put everyone on half-time; pass around a questionnaire to see who would be most willing to work with fewer accounts, and so forth. Then, from those suggestions, group members discussed preferred alternatives. The result was a part-time schedule for most employees, except for a few individuals with heavy family obligations, and a feeling of pulling together to help the company weather the storm.

Mary L. Got the Job She Wanted by Brainstorming

In another case, Mary L. wasn't sure what career path to take. She wasn't clear about what skills she had, and she felt, based on her many interests, that she could go in many directions. Eventually, after several weeks of gazing over the classifieds, answering ads, being turned down, and feeling more and more confused, Mary tried brainstorming to think more clearly about the skills she had, decide which skills she wanted to use in a job, and write up a new résumé reflecting this.

She started off by asking herself the question: "What can I do?" and quickly wrote down everything she could think of on a list. When she slowed down, she asked the question again: "What else can I do?" She kept asking, until nothing else came.

Next, reviewing the list, she asked herself for each skill—"Do I want to use this on a job?" Then, she rated each skill with a 1 (very much), 2 (maybe), and 3 (no), and crossed off all the 3s. Finally, going through the list again, she asked the question: "What have I done using this skill?" and she wrote down everything she could think of.

With this information she at last had a clear sense of what she wanted to do and what she had done, and she wrote up a new résumé featuring the skills she wanted to use, along with examples of past jobs or volunteer situations in which she had used these skills. Then, with this new focus, she zeroed in on the kind of job she really wanted—an administrative assistant job in a management consulting firm, so she could get the background to move into management consulting herself. With this knowledge, she answered a few ads, and within a few days had exactly the job she wanted.

Both these examples are of people who have used their creativity to discover solutions to problems and make decisions through a process known as brainstorming. This process involves two stages. In the first stage, an individual or group of people come up with as many alternative ideas or problem solutions as quickly as possible. In the second, they select the most appropriate ideas from this list and seek to implement them.

The brainstorming process is extremely valuable for increasing creativity, because it triggers your mind power abilities to start generating new ideas and solutions, without any restrictive attempts to evaluate them. That's why this is a two stage process—the first to generate ideas; the second to review them critically to eliminate those that don't work and prioritize those that are possible.

The technique has become a popular problem-solving technique used for numerous purposes, including structuring organizations, resolving interpersonal conflicts and making career and management decisions. The process works very effectively in a group with a leader who directs the process by first encouraging people to shout out ideas, writes them down, and then asks people to vote on the ideas they like.

You can similarly use brainstorming by first directing your imagination to generate as many ideas as possible and writing them down. Then go over these ideas critically to select out the best ones to attain your goal.

Combining Brainstorming with Relaxation and Visualization Techniques

I use the process myself constantly, and frequently combine it with some of the relaxation and visualization techniques described earlier. For instance, as a game designer, I have used brainstorming, in addition to the extended mental journeys to toy stores described earlier, to come up with dozens of game ideas, about two dozen of which have ended up on the market. Often I started this process to generate ideas by looking at some materials I happened to have in my workshop (such as some long screws and plastic spheres I acquired without knowing what I would do with them and asking myself: "What are all the possible things I can create with these objects?" Then, I would let my mind powers go to work, and I would write down all the images that came (such as, place the bolts in a circle on a piece of wood and throw the sphere into it; make a large hole in the sphere and aim the bolts at it). Finally, I would select the ideas I considered workable and create a game or puzzle design based on that. (For instance, I eventually turned the spheres and bolts into a puzzle that involved taking different sized bolts out of the sphere and trying to put them back in again so they all fit. Subsequently I sold this idea to Hasbro Industries which produced about 100,000 puzzles under the name *Screwball*.)

Similarly, with clients who come to me about marketing or organizational problems, I simply turn on my creative mind, focus it on the problem and facts they have presented to me, and brainstorm as many alternative solutions as possible. I tell my client I am coming up with ideas "off the top of my head," and indicate we can decide on the best alternative later. But, for now, we only want to think about the possibilities, so I phrase my question to reflect this and ask something like: "How many ways can I..." (solve the problem; create a new organizational structure; get to a goal?")

As an example, one client wasn't sure how to market a new personalized soap product. So we started brainstorming in a number of areas: "Who are all the groups of people who might use this soap?" "What are some names that might appeal to them?" "What are all the marketing outlets that might sell this soap?" Afterwards, we selected the most likely marketing targets, the most appealing name, and the primary marketing outlets to reach this group.

Another client wanted to make a career decision: Should she go into nursing or research? So together, we brainstormed all the advantages and disadvantages of choosing nursing for her, and I wrote them down as she came up with them. Then, we brainstormed all the advantages and disadvantages of research. After this, I asked her to rate her advantages on a plus scale of 1 to 5 and her disadvantages on a minus scale of 1 to 5 and add them up. Finally, I asked her to divide the results by the total number of advantages and disadvantages on each list and compare the results for nursing and research. She found that nursing came out with a much higher score, and after we talked about her feelings towards the two professions a little more to confirm what the rating system indicated, she opted to go to nursing school. Now, about two years later, she is close to graduating and feels confident her decision was right.

You can use brainstorming similarly to solve problems and make decisions creatively. The key is letting your mind go so your intuitive abilities generate ideas. Then you evaluate them later using your logical mind. The techniques described in this chapter are designed to help you do this.

HOW TO USE BRAINSTORMING

The following techniques are based on the two-stage principle of brainstorming:

1. You give your imagination and intuition free rein as you think of as many ideas as you can.

2. You review these ideas critically to decide which are best or which are appropriate for further developments.

You can use this process to come up with alternative possibilities for just about anything from a small object to a complex long-term undertaking. You can use it to resolve your uncertainty about a situation or come up with creative ideas generally.

The following two techniques will help you limber up your mental processes, so you start generating alternatives. If there is a special issue you are concerned about, choose that to work with (such as: how to make your company or department more profitable, get a product on the market, or get people to join your organization). Or choose a hypothetical problem to gain skill at using the process, so you can readily apply your ability to something else. You can work with a group of people and brainstorm about a common issue, or use these techniques on your own.

---

1. FINDING SOLUTIONS AND ALTERNATIVES   Time: 5-10 minutes

If you are doing this technique yourself, take a sheet of paper and a pencil, and at the top write down a problem you want to solve or an objective you want to achieve. If you are doing this in a group, appoint one person the leader, and have him or her write down the problem or objective on a blackboard or flip chart.

This problem or objective can be a physical one, such as building a house or designing a product; an organizational issue, such as creating a more effective sales group; a process question, such as how to publicize or market a new program; a personal matter, such as getting a better job or promotion; or a hypothetical goal, like what to do if you suddenly receive a $10,000 bonus at work.

Next, divide your sheet of paper, blackboard, or flip chart into three columns, headed respectively: Approaches, Persons, and Objects. Then, for each column, ask yourself the following questions.

- *What are all the ways I can solve this problem? or What are all the alternative methods I can use to do this project?*
- *Who are the people or groups I need to make this happen?*
- *What are the objects I need to achieve this goal?*

As you ask each question, write down whatever comes, or if you are working in a group call it out and your leader will write it down. Don't try to evaluate. Just let the ideas pop into your head and make a record of them.

After five minutes, review your list critically to determine which approaches are the best and which persons or items you really need. Circle the ones that you consider good possibilities, and cross out those that clearly are not. Then, rank the circled ideas in order of priority. If there are too many ideas to rank them immediately, mark the best ones with a 1; the next group with a 2; and the least favorable with a 3. Then, you can rank the 1s, 2s, and 3s in turn. If you are working with a group, do this rating process by taking votes.

2. FINDING A USE FOR WHAT YOU HAVE   Time: 10-15 minutes

Another productive type of brainstorming is coming up with uses for things you already have on hand. This is the reverse of coming up with what you need to do or have to acquire to solve a problem or achieve a goal. Rather, you are creating an objective or goal for yourself to make use of the resources you currently have.

This approach is especially useful for expanding your productivity; increasing the activities of your organization; or coming up with new inventions or products. You're innovating in every sense of the word—and the results can be extremely profitable, as you're starting with what you already have.

Again, you can do this technique by yourself or work with a group. Start by writing down some overall goal or purpose at the top of a sheet of paper, such as: "Creating a popular new doll or game," or "New projects my company or department can do." Next, make two columns on a sheet of paper, blackboard, or flip chart and head them: "What I Have to Use" and "How I Can Use What I Have." Then, divide your paper into three sections, and at the far left, title each section respectively: "Persons," "Talents and Skills," and "Objects."

Now start coming up with ideas to attain your goal by filling in the boxes. Begin with the column "What I Have to Use." As quickly as possible, with your goal in mind, list all the persons, talents and skills, and objects you have available and want to use. Don't try to evaluate how these might be used. Just write down whatever comes to mind, and take about five minutes to do this.

For instance, suppose you are brainstorming about a new career for yourself. You would write down "myself" under persons, and next think about the skills you want to employ (for example, writing, organizing, managing). Lastly, you might consider if there are any objects you want to use (such as a typewriter, camera, word processor) and list these.

If you are trying to come up with a new invention, you might list some of the individuals you may need to work with, such as a patent attorney, plastics engineer, and printer. Then, after skipping the section for talents and skills, you might list some objects you have in your office or workshop that you could include in this invention, such as "plastic pieces," "steel balls," and "chrome wire."

After you have filled in what you have and want to use in the first column, look at each item in turn and think of all the ways you might use it to reach your goal. Again, don't evaluate. Just write. (Or call out ideas if you're in a group). If nothing comes right away, go on to the next item. Afterward, go back to any mental blanks and try one more time.

CHART # 8

	What I Have to Use	How I Can Use What I Have
Persons		
Talents & Skills		
Objects		

Finally, it's time to evaluate and choose. If any approach you have listed seems useful, circle it. If you have solved the problem or have fully achieved your purpose, you are done. Or try another round of brainstorming if additional details remain to be worked out.

In using this technique, ideally select a purpose that you feel is useful to you. Should you have trouble coming up with something, you can use some of the suggestions below to get you used to brainstorming creatively. Then apply the process to your own purposes. The basic principle is the same and works with any situation—by brainstorming freely about new approaches for using what you have, you can come up with new directions and solutions. In effect, you're building a better mousetrap with what you have.

For example, some possible purposes and things you have on hand might be:

Desired Purpose: New markets for a manufactured product
             New services my company can offer
             New products I can make with my current
             manufacturing plant

What I Have to Use:
Objects: *The product I am making*
             Fiberboard squares, plastic boxes
             Printing press, copying machine
Persons: *Myself*
             Sales Manager, Marketing Manager, Research and
             Development Director
             Art, Paul, Susie, Tom, and Me
Talents/Skills: Word Processing
             Writing, Advertising, Publicity
             Cooking, Fund Raising, Art Work

Now start thinking about what you have that you want to use for some purpose. You'll start thinking more creatively immediately—and you'll increase your productivity, efficiency, effectiveness, and profits as a result.

 *Chapter 12*

Making Right Decisions Using Your Intuition

Coming up with a variety of alternatives and selecting the best one (as described in Chapter 11) can be one way to reach a decision. But sometimes you have difficulty choosing among the alternatives, or there may be no alternatives—only the option of saying yes, no, or deferring the decision to a later time when you are more ready to decide. For instance, you are presented with a new job offer or a promotion requiring a move. Should you take it or not? You see an expensive computer that might help your business. Should you buy now or wait? You have visited several possible locations for your company. Which one should you take?

Sometimes it's hard to decide, and you don't feel you have the ability or time to work out your decision logically by weighing all the pros and cons and then deciding. In fact, logic can sometimes get in the way of making the right gut-level decision that satisfies your inner self.

That's when it helps to tap directly into your unconscious or intuition to make that gut-level choice that expresses what you really want. As it's sometimes difficult to hear that inner voice, the exercises in this chapter are designed to help you both trigger that inner response and listen to what it says to do.

HOW INTUITION TECHNIQUES WORK

These techniques work by altering your consciousness, so that you pay attention to your unconscious or intuition and respond accordingly. In turn, your intuition can talk to you in a number of ways—through automatic writing, through visual symbols or thoughts, through signals from your body. Different people get their information in different ways—and the way you get information may change under different circumstances.

For example, I commonly use automatic writing for making more important decisions, such as choosing among different work projects, when I can't do everything and must make a choice. Also, I call on this ability only occasionally, perhaps once or twice a month, so it retains its specialness for me. When I use it, I typically take a minute or two to get relaxed, ask a question, and write down whatever answers I receive. After this first question, my writing takes the form of a dialogue between me and my inner voice, and I write down whatever it says. For instance, it might say something like:

> You're thinking of doing too many projects right now. There's a risk of getting scattered and doing nothing very well. So choose. We know it's difficult. But select the project you feel is most important to you.
>
> What is it that you ask? Well, for right now, we think...

Afterwards, I read over what I have written and use this advice to make a decision, and usually do what my writing has advised.

Also, from time to time, I read over past messages and review them in light of the outcome that resulted when I followed the advice. It's a way of further verifying the value of the technique by looking back to see that I have gotten good advice—which I usually have.

Some people prefer to get advice by going on mental journeys or by mentally asking a counselor for assistance. For instance, one associate, Pam G., imagines herself entering a workshop in her home where she has a computer console. She presses a button and an image of her counselor appears on the monitor. He looks a little like a college professor of physics, with a thin face, small goatee, graying hair, and pipe. Then, she asks him questions and the answers appear on the screen.

One time she consulted with her counselor when she wasn't sure whether to leave her word processing job to try freelancing as a computer consultant. His advice: be patient and start working freelance on a part-time basis. Another time, she was considering making a major purchase of a computer system for her freelance business, and her counselor suggested that she should rent first and later consider buying when her business was big enough.

Another associate, Andrea S., often takes a long mental trip to see an old man on a mountain for advice. She begins by seeing herself in a beautiful meadow and then walks along a path that leads through the woods into the mountains. After a while, she comes to a small mountain cabin and inside meets a wise man who knows the answers to whatever she asks. He invites her in for tea, and as they drink it, she asks him questions about whatever problems are confronting her at work or in her life generally—such as: "How can I get my boss to treat me more seriously?" or "Where should I go on my vacation?" Then, she listens to the answer, thanks the old man, and leaves.

What these examples illustrate is that all of these methods of communicating with your intuition work. The key is to choose a technique that works for you—or even create your own mental journey to unlock your intuition, so it gives you answers and insights.

You can also get quick answers as you go through the day with other techniques. For example, sometimes I'll want an immediate "yes" or "no" decision. Should I rent a room in my house to a person? Should I loan a friend some money? Should I go to a business meeting or should I stay home and work on a project?

Such questions come up for everyone dozens of times a day, and obviously, you can't take the time to use an extended visualization to discover an answer. You need to make your decision immediately.

In such cases, I seek an answer to a question one of two ways—and sometimes, I even get the answer before I have fully asked the question. It happens that fast. The first way I get an answer is by seeing it on a screen in my mind or listening for my little voice to give me a "yes," "no," or short message. I ask my question—or sometimes I just feel it, without putting it into words—and then I wait for the answer to appear on the screen in whatever form it comes. Sometimes it will be a single word flashing on the screen; sometimes a color (green for "yes"; red for "no"; yellow for "not sure right now"); and sometimes the word "yes" or "no" resounding in my head like a beeper.

Other people tend to get messages directly from their body. For example, when they get a yes, they feel a slight quickening of their pulse, experience a vibrancy in their chest and stomach, and sense their heart beating faster. One associate uses his body like a pendulum. When his body sways forward and back ever so slightly, he knows it's saying yes; when it swings to the right and left, he knows the answer is no; and when he sways in circles, he feels he isn't sure. The movements are so small that other people can't detect them; but he can feel them, and in an instant, he knows what to do.

The following techniques illustrate how you can use these methods to tap into your own unconscious. These methods include automatic writing, taking a journey in your imagination, asking your counselor for advice, and getting answers from your mental screen, inner voice, or body. Use whichever approach works best for you in a particular situation.

MAKING AN IMPORTANT DECISION

The following three techniques—automatic writing, taking a journey in your imagination, and asking your counselor for advice—are three methods for making an important decision or getting answers to questions you have. As these techniques require you to take time to be quietly with yourself, I recommend using them only occasionally, and using the quick decision methods described in the next section on an everyday basis.

You may find you have more of an affinity to one of these techniques than the others. If so, use that. Or vary the techniques you use, depending on the situation and what feels right at the time.

For all of these techniques find a place where you can get relaxed and comfortable. Close your eyes if you like.

---

1. MAKING THE WRITE DECISION   Time: 10-20 minutes

In this technique, you'll use automatic writing to learn what you need to know. To set the stage, have paper and pencil available, or put a sheet of paper in a typewriter so you can immediately begin to type. Perhaps use a notebook to keep track of your communications on a regular basis.

It also helps to create a comfortable writing environment that will help to alter your consciousness. For instance, use candles or other dim lighting, and, if you like, put on some background music—preferably something soft and easy to listen to.

Then, use a relaxation technique to alter your state of consciousness, such as concentrating on your breathing or focusing on a single word like "om" or "relax." Once you feel spacey, you are ready to begin writing. Turn off any music, because you need quiet to concentrate.

Now ask any questions about your decision mentally or write them down. "What should I do?" "What is in my best interest?" "What would I like to do?" "What are my alternatives?" "Which alternatives would I prefer?" And so on.... Then wait for your answer. It may come to you as a voice in your head, or it may seem like a communication from a spirit guide or a being with a personality. Either way, write down your answer as it comes. Don't think or analyze. Just write. Keep asking questions and recording answers until the questions and responses stop.

Finally, review what you have written. The course you want to take should be clear.

2. ASKING YOUR COUNSELOR FOR ADVICE   Time: 10-15 minutes

In this technique, you'll use a computer and a monitor or a movie screen to contact an expert counselor who knows all the answers.

Imagine that you have a special workshop or office in your house where you can go to find out whatever you want to know. It may be in the attic or the basement; perhaps it is a new addition in the garage; or maybe it used to be a bedroom.

Wherever it is, go to it and take your time getting there. Notice what is around you as you walk there, and when you are ready, open the door and go inside. As you enter, look around. There are all kinds of books and papers. You see large stacks of computer printouts.

Then, at the far wall, you notice a long desk and above it a computer console, with numerous gadgets and buttons to press. Above this you see a large monitor that looks like a movie screen. Just press a button and you can see a movie of your own experiences on this screen.

Now, to work on resolving some problem or getting advice, press the button and you'll see the situation that you want to resolve unfold on the screen. Or you may see the question you want to ask appear.

Once the problem or question is clear, you can seek a solution or answer. To obtain this, press a button to stop the movie and press another to summon your counselor. He or she will appear on the screen with advice for you. Your counselor may be someone you know—or possibly your counselor just looks like someone who is very knowledgeable. Whoever it is, welcome your counselor and ask for help. Tell him or her what is wrong and ask for advice on what to do or say to resolve matters.

Now listen as your counselor tells you what to do. If the answer is simple, he or she will reply briefly, or your counselor may ask you to press a button on your console so you can see the solution. Then, some action you can take will appear on the screen.

If you have more questions, continue to ask them and your counselor will reply. Again, wait for your answer in whatever form it comes. When you have no more questions, tell your counselor you are done, and his or her image will disappear from the screen.

Then, turn off your computer console and leave your workshop. Return to the regular part of your house, and as you do, return to normal consciousness and open your eyes.

Usually, you will have clear answers as a result of this process. However, if your counselor has no answers or asks you to wait, this means you don't have enough information or the situation is unclear. If so, perhaps wait a few days and ask your questions again; or use some of the other techniques described in this book to obtain more information or increase your confidence, so you are in a better position to take action.

3. TAKING A JOURNEY TO FIND THE ANSWER   Time 10-20 minutes

In this technique, you'll take a journey up to the top of a mountain to learn your answers from the wise old man or woman of the mountain. To take this journey you need to be very relaxed and comfortable. You can best use this technique in two ways. One way is to read this description first and use it to guide your experience in a general way; or record the journey on tape and play it back while you listen. The following guide uses a wise man. Substitute a wise woman if you prefer.

This journey begins in the midst of a beautiful meadow. See yourself there surrounded by lush green foliage. The air is clear and warmed by the sun. Nearby, you hear the subtle buzz of bees and the chatter of birds. Off in the distance you see a large mountain and walk towards it. As you walk, notice the tiny flowers. Little mushrooms pop up in the shade of trees. You can feel the carpet of moss beneath your feet. Cows grazing on the hillside low softly.

As you walk towards the mountain, the trees begin to thin out and you pass patches of grassland. The wind feels stronger and cooler. Now you pass a small stream. Sit down for a moment. Let your feet dangle in the stream. Feel the water move past them. It's so relaxing. You feel very peaceful. Now sit very still and listen. Notice the infinite variety of movements around you. Dragonflies make darting passes as they skim the stream. A crab crawls out from under a stone seeking a better place to hide. Tadpoles swim by, and above your head birds fly from perch to perch. Squirrels race up a tree. Insects balance themselves on blades of grass. Nearby, a deer stands quietly watching. Sit on a large rock, and look around you. What else do you see?

Now go on. As you walk uphill, note that the trees give way to bushes. You come to a clearing and look down on the meadow and valley below. Notice how far away it seems—like another world.

Now as you climb higher and higher, notice how the air begins to cool. Yet the sun shines on you directly and warms you. Then as you climb on, experience a sense of clarity and self-understanding, as you get farther and farther away from the things that usually concern you. It is as if you are leaving the world and all its cares behind. Realizing this, you feel an intense sense of peace.

Now you come near the top of the mountain. At the top, there is a small hut made of intricately carved wood. The windows and doorways are hung with mirrors and small objects that flash and shine in the light.

This is where the wise man of the mountain lives. He is said to know about everything. You approach the cabin. As you do, think of the questions you wish to have answered. Think of the decision you have to make and select your most important question to ask first.

Now, with your question clearly in mind, go up to the door and knock three times. The wise man will answer. As he opens the door, he asks you: "What question do you bring?" In response, look him in the eyes and clearly state your question. As you do, observe him closely. Notice his eyes; the way he is dressed. He looks like a seer, who knows the answers to all things.

Then, he invites you into his cabin to share tea. As you drink it, he tells you the answer to your question. Listen as he answers your question now. If you have additional questions, ask them after he finishes his answer.

Afterward, thank him for his answers. Talk of other things if you like and stay as long as you wish. When you say goodbye, go back down the mountain as you came, and return to the meadow where you began your journey.

MAKING A QUICK DECISION

These next two techniques are designed to give you quick answers to a simple question. In one you pose your question mentally and wait for a quick response from your mental screen or inner voice. In the second, you turn your body into a pendulum and get your answer from the way your body moves.

Use these techniques whenever you need a quick yes or no about something or you have a simple choice to make between a limited number of alternatives.

---

1. GETTING YOUR ANSWER FROM YOUR
   MENTAL SCREEN OR INNER VOICE   Time 1-10 minutes

This technique is used to get an immediate "yes," "no," or "not certain" answer, or to make a quick choice where you decide between "this" or "that."

To use this technique effectively, you have to do some preliminary conditioning to get your mental screen or inner voice ready to respond immediately. But once you've laid this groundwork, you can use this technique without further rehearsals, as long as you use it regularly—at least a few times a week.

To establish this conditioning, get relaxed and comfortable in a quiet place. Then, start by asking yourself some yes-no questions to which you already know the answer, such as: "Was I born in 1935?" "Did I work at Sears, Roebuck and Co.?"

Now, notice how you get your answer. You may hear a yes or no in your mind; you may see a yes or no appear in your mind's eye; or perhaps you may see a flash or color, such as green for yes and red for no. However this response comes, concentrate on getting your future answers the same way, so you develop that method of getting answers.

Then, continue to ask yourself questions to which you know the answers and work on getting your response to come more quickly, until you hear or see it as a quick flash. Finally, ask yourself a few questions to which you don't know the answer, and ask your intuition to give you the appropriate response. For example, if you are seeing the words "yes" and "no" appear, you should see "maybe" or "not sure" appear. If you are hearing the words, you should hear "maybe" or "not sure." If you are seeing color flashes, you should see a yellow flash for uncertainty.

Condition yourself to make choices in the same way. Start by thinking about a choice you have already made, and imagine the options you had when you made the choice. Then, as you think of the choice you actually made, see the word or phrase describing that choice appear on the mental screen in your mind's eye, or hear your inner voice say this word or phrase, or, perhaps, see an image or symbol representing this choice.

Again, note the way in which you receive your answer, and concentrate on getting future answers the same way. Then, continue to ask yourself to select choices you have already made, and concentrate on getting your response to appear more quickly. Finally, ask yourself to make a few simple choices that you haven't made before, and if you aren't ready to choose, see or hear the word you have previously used to express uncertainty.

Continue to practice this technique regularly for about a week until you feel it has become a part of your life. Then, start using it to get answers as you go about your everyday life.

You'll find the answers start popping up automatically on your mental screen or you'll hear them spoken by your inner voice.

2. ASKING YOUR BODY FOR ANSWERS   Time 1-10 minutes

An alternate way to get yes, no, and maybe answers is by asking your body, as your body holds the key to your subconscious when you learn to read your body cues and train your body to give those cues.

As with the mental screen and inner voice techniques, you need to do some initial practice to train your responses until they become automatic. In this case, you must physically move your body to get your answers, but after some practice, you can visualize these bodily movements in your mind or can develop a voice inside you to answer for your body. Alternatively, you can learn to feel very subtle motions within your body, such as the speed of your pulse or your heartbeat.

One way to get started asking your body for information is to train your body to act like a pendulum, which will move forward and back to give you "yes" answers; to the side to give you "nos", and in a circle to give you "maybes" or "not sures." To condition your body to respond this way, use the following technique.

Stand straight and imagine your body as a pendulum. Now sway backward and forward. That means "yes." Sway to the right and left. That means "no." Sway in a circular motion. That means you are familiar with the signals. Then ask yourself some simple yes-no questions to which you know the answers. Your body should respond with the appropriate swaying motion. Once it does this consistently, you are ready to begin asking it for answers.

Ask your questions as yes-no questions, and phrase them as follows: "Is it in my best interest to do such and such?" not, "Should I do it?" You want to do what you want or need to do—what's best for you—not what you should. After you ask, observe how your body responds—with a yes motion, a no, or a maybe. With practice, you should get clear yeses and nos. Once you do, you can decide whether to act accordingly.

If you get a lot of circular motions (maybes) or get alternating yeses and nos to the same question, you may not be asking the question clearly, or your personality may be getting in the way. To find out, simply ask: "Is my question unclear?" Or "Is my personality getting in the way?" If so, either clarify or reframe your question, or push your conscious thoughts and feelings aside to let your inner self speak. Or ask your question another time.

At first, you will have to physically assume this pendulum position when you ask a question. But once you are familiar with this technique and consistently get clear answers, you can make it a mental process. Just imagine your body as a pendulum and ask your question. Then observe how your body responds in your mind's eye, or listen to what your inner voice tells you about your body.

Later, you won't need to imagine the pendulum. You can merely ask your question and feel your body respond with a yes or a no.

 *Chapter 13*

Improve Your Health and Eliminate Bad Habits

Having good health and habits plays a critical part in your business success, as they contribute a productive, high-quality performance. When you feel well, you do well, for you have the energy and ability to concentrate your powers on the task at hand, without the distractions of health problems or annoying habits.

In turn, your mind powers can help you feel better and chase away simple ailments, like a cold or sore throat. They can also help you break bad habits, such as smoking or overeating. Of course, if anything is seriously wrong, see a doctor and use your mind power abilities along with medical supervision, as this book is not a medical guide. But for everyday problems, the mind power techniques have proved helpful for several people whose stories I share here.

Ward Off Colds Through the Power of Your Mind

For example, in the winter, Don J., a graphics designer, used to come down with frequent colds and sore throats, which kept him off the job, because he was afraid of coming down with something worse. When he got the first sign of a cold—usually a strange tightness in his throat—he believed the cold was inevitable, and he awaited its coming in a day or two, like an unwelcome visitor he felt he couldn't turn away.

145

But then, a few years ago, after attending a workshop on the powers of the mind, he began using his mind powers to ward off these illnesses. He started taking action as soon as he felt the first symptom of a cold or sore throat coming on. He sat down in a chair in his living room, closed his eyes, visualized healing energy pouring into himself from the earth and air around him, and saw this energy form into a bright white beam, which he directed at the twinge of pain in his throat or head. Meanwhile, he thought to himself: "You will remain healthy. You will not get a cold. Your sore throat will go away."

Over the next few days, he continued this visualization a few times a day, until he felt the danger of getting ill was past. The result was that most of the time Don was able to avoid coming down with colds or sore throats that he felt sure he would have gotten otherwise. And the few times he did come down with something, he noticed it was much less severe than usual—only a day or two of symptoms that kept him in bed feeling miserable, compared to three or four days before he started practicing these exercises. Further, he noticed that the times he did come down with something he hadn't been doing these exercises on a regular basis.

Losing Weight—Harriet G.'s Success Story

In another case, Harriet G., a teacher, used these techniques to get control of her weight. She had been battling the problem for several years, trying one diet after another, without much success. She would lose a few pounds, start approaching her ideal weight of 125, and then lose her commitment to stay on her diet. After about five years of this, she was close to giving up and becoming resigned to being about twenty pounds higher than she wanted to be, when she heard about the value of mind power techniques.

After finding a quiet comfortable place in her house, she began using these techniques by meditating on the reason she was having so much trouble staying on a diet. "Why can't I keep my weight down?" she asked her unconscious. "You need a reminder," her inner voice replied, "and you need to find ways to reward yourself each day for being good."

She continued to dialogue with this voice for a while, and finally it told her a specific program to follow for the next two weeks. She should meditate briefly twice a day and affirm to herself: "You don't need to eat so much. You can eat less and you won't feel hungry." She should concentrate on having mainly liquids, vegetables, and fruits. She should have a protein drink for breakfast instead of a regular meal. And especially important, she should "take a pill, any pill, with your meal to remind yourself you are on a diet and you need to exercise control. As you're already taking vitamin pills, use them. These will remind you to stop eating once you have had enough, and you will lose weight."

She started her diet the next day, and by the end of the week had lost four pounds. And this time, with the help of her mind and continued meditation on what to do next, her weight stayed down for the next few weeks.

Quick Recovery from an Accident

Similarly Judy L. used these techniques to recover quickly from an accident and get right back to work. She was in the middle of organizing her house and office to prepare for a move, when she slipped and fell so her head hit the side of her stereo speaker. She didn't feel much pain, so she didn't realize it was serious until she started noticing spatters of blood on the floor and felt drops rolling down her cheeks.

At this point, many people might have gotten upset and excited. But she didn't. Instead, she simply looked to her mind powers to help her know what to do. Calmly she asked herself questions like: "What do I do now?" and listened to her answers. Meanwhile, she kept her major goal in mind—as she had so many things to do, she needed to take care of the situation as quickly as possible, so she could return to work and make the deadline.

The result of this inner dialogue was that she calmly lay down, held some tissue to her head, and focused on stopping the flow of blood. She visualized the blood vessels in her head constricting and the blood slowing down, and in a few minutes the bleeding stopped. Then, still calm, relaxed, and feeling no pain, she lay down for about fifteen minutes to ride out the initial shock reaction that was making her feel woozy, and she concentrated on those feelings going away. Once they were gone, she calmly called the emergency room at the hospital, drove herself there, and when the doctors put in eleven stitches to close up the large gash in her forehead, she saw herself floating outside her body, looking down on the process. Meanwhile, she kept thinking about her goal—to get home and back to work as quickly as possible.

As a result, the procedure went very quickly. She experienced practically no pain, and about four hours after the accident, she was back at work. Within a few days, the stitches were removed, and after another week, it was like the accident never happened.

By contrast, I know other people who have had accidents that could have been similarly handled in a few hours. But these accidents have precipitated major life crises, not because of the accident itself, but because of their reaction to it. For instance, Sarah S., a teacher in her 50s slipped in her bedroom, had a hairline fracture of one of her hips, was put in a cast for a few weeks, and ended up in and out of hospitals for about two years afterwards, because her negative attitude unleashed all sorts of fears, which led her to see herself as an invalid and feel suicidal, rather than focusing on quickly getting well.

In short, the message I want to emphasize is that illnesses, accidents, and bad habits happen. But by having a positive attitude and mobilizing your inner forces to quickly combat the problem, you can readily improve your productivity, performance, and enjoyment of life.

The techniques in this chapter show you how to do this.

HOW MIND POWER TECHNIQUES IMPROVE YOUR HEALTH AND HABITS

These mind power techniques can help you feel better and get rid of bad habits, because the vast majority of our illnesses and bad habits have some mental or psychological basis. For example, feeling stress is a mental response to some situation, and numerous illnesses and bad conditions develop in response to stress. Also, stress lowers our resistance to certain diseases, so we may come down with something, usually in that part of our body that is the weakest. For instance, after experiencing stress some people come down with a cold; some with stomach cramps; others with a headache. Thus, using any relaxation technique (as described in Chapter 3) can help your health generally by reducing stress.

Our expectations also influence whether we stay well or get sick. For instance, if you're around someone with a cold or get chilled, you may expect consciously or unconsciously to catch something—and if you expect it, you often will get what you expect. However, you can counteract or reverse your expectations by setting up a mental shield before you encounter a situation that could cause problems or by using a mental cleansing process afterwards.

Yet even with such precautions, sometimes we all get sick or feel the telltale symptoms that warn us we may be coming down with something, such as feeling the dizziness that sometimes precedes the flu. In this case, you can send healing energy to the part of your body at risk, so you may be able to reverse the process—or at least make the ensuing illness less serious.

Then, if you do get ill, your mind powers can make you feel better while recovering and speed your recovery. You see yourself feeling better and affirm you are getting better, too.

Finally, you can use your mind power abilities to do a routine body check, and if you notice any weak spots, you can send healing energy there to possibly avoid a subsequent illness or problem.

In the case of habits, these mind power techniques work by interrupting your normally unconscious tendency to respond according to habit. Instead, you make yourself very aware you have a habit by paying attention to it and reminding yourself that you have it each time you do it, so you can mentally decide to stop doing it. At the same time, you repeatedly see yourself without that habit or you visualize that habit as undesirable and repulsive.

However, to break a habit, you must really want to change, not just think you do. Thus, before you start using your mind powers to break a habit, you have to examine your real desires to be sure you really want to change. Once you are certain, you can direct your mind powers to that goal by working on reprogramming your mind. It may take some time to change the programming, as a habit has become part of your unconscious. So even if you stop doing something, such as smoking, the longing can stay with you for some time. Yet with commitment and persistence you can make those old urges go away, and your mind power abilities can speed up the process.

The following techniques demonstrate how. The first set of techniques deal with improving your health and the healing process. The second set help you break bad habits.

IMPROVE YOUR HEALTH AND SPEED UP THE HEALING PROCESS

The following techniques provide procedures for handling several common health situations:

- getting rid of stress
- protecting yourself from exposure to an illness
- preventing yourself from getting ill
- getting rid of headaches

- making a faster and more comfortable recovery
- discovering potential weak spots in your body and strengthening them

Feel free to adapt each approach to your own needs or apply the basic principles to create other visualizations for other health problems. However, be sure to see a doctor if the condition persist.

---

1. GETTING RID OF STRESS

To get rid of stress, use your mind powers to direct yourself to relax. You can use the exercises described in Chapter 3 to overcome this common problem.

2. PROTECTING YOURSELF FROM EXPOSURE TO AN ILLNESS   Time: 1-2 minutes

You can protect yourself from exposure to an illness with your mind powers in two ways. One is to mentally shield yourself in advance if you are going to be in a place where someone is ill or shield yourself immediately on encountering this person. For example, if you go to the office, and someone has a bad cold, this is the time to protect yourself with this technique.

The other way to protect yourself is to cleanse yourself mentally after being exposed if you don't have time to create your mental shield before your exposure. You can cleanse yourself while you are still with the person or as soon after you have been exposed as possible. Then, if you remain in the area of exposure, you can put up your mental shield after cleansing to continue your protection. If you leave the area, you won't need it.

Beside protecting you from illness, these shielding and cleansing techniques can also protect you from negative people and situations. Use the shield to fend off any negativity, and use the cleansing approach to clear away any negativity.

• SHIELDING YOURSELF:

To use the shielding technique, visualize a shield of white light around yourself when you feel threatened by an illness or any negativity. See this shield radiating from the center of your head and surrounding you completely. This shield provides a ring of protection around you, so that if any germs or negative forces hit this shield, they bounce right off. When you leave the area or no longer feel threatened, release the shield and it will dissolve.

● CLEANSING YOURSELF:

To use the cleansing technique, visualize yourself standing in a small room, surrounded by brilliant white light. Now experience the light pouring down around you like purifying water. As it does, lift your hands and brush any impurities from all parts of your body, as if you were cleansing yourself in a shower. Then, when you feel clean, step out of the shower of light, feeling protected and refreshed.

3. PREVENTING YOURSELF FROM GETTING ILL   Time: 3-5 minutes

When you first feel you are getting sick—such as experiencing the sore throat that appears before you come down with a cold—you can send healing energy to that affected part to possibly reverse the process of getting ill or make the illness less serious. This technique is one way to mobilize and direct this healing energy. Ideally, find a quiet place, get comfortable, and close your eyes.

Visualize a radiant bubble of healing energy around you. Energy flows into this bubble from the earth and the air around you, and then brilliant white healing energy flows into you from this bubble.

Feel this beam of energy pouring into you, and direct it to your affected part. Now feel this healing warmth and energy flowing into that area and healing it, so you feel fine.

Continue to hold this image for several minutes. As you do, experience more and more healing energy being transferred into the affected area, and the area continuing to feel better and better. Finally, release the energy, and it will retract back into the bubble, and then dissipate back into the earth and the air.

Do this technique several times a day, possibly for a few days, until you feel that the signs of an impending illness are completely gone.

4. GETTING RID OF HEADACHES   Time: 3-5 minutes

A good technique for getting rid of headaches is mentally zapping them with a laser beam, rather than using the healing bubble technique. Again, it is best to get quiet and comfortable, close your eyes, and experience getting rid of your headache for several minutes.

To begin, focus your attention on your headache. Notice where it is and visualize its shape. Now project this shape in front of you. Continue to hold it in front of you. As you do, visualize a laser beam of light coming from your head and going into your headache. As the light streams in, the headache begins to shatter and dissolve. Continue focusing the light on your headache as it disintegrates. Then when it is gone or feels better, turn off the laser and open your eyes.

5. MAKING A FASTER AND MORE
COMFORTABLE RECOVERY   Time: 3-5 minutes

To feel better and get better faster, focus your attention on getting well. In addition, you can have a dialogue with your inner self to find out if there is anything special you should do to speed your recovery. This technique illustrates how to do both.

To get started, relax, close your eyes, and ask yourself: "What should I do to speed my recovery?" Then, listen to the answer, and ask more questions if you need to, so you get any instructions you need. Later, keep this advice in mind while you are recovering.

Next, see yourself participating in your everyday activities and being completely well. For instance, you are back at work feeling fine, and you are doing whatever you normally do at work effectively and productively. Hold this image for several minutes, and as you do, repeat to yourself: "I am well. I am well. I am well." or "I feel fine. I feel fine."

When you open your eyes, you should feel better already. Do this exercise several times a day to speed your recovery.

6. DISCOVERING POTENTIAL WEAK SPOTS IN
YOUR BODY AND STRENGTHENING THEM   Time: 5-10 minutes

Sometimes there are weak spots in your body of which you may not be aware. You can use your mind powers to discover if there are any, and if so, where they are. Then, you can send healing energy to strengthen them, using the bubble technique described in Technique 3—Preventing Yourself From Getting Ill.

To check out your body, take a mental trip through your circulation system and cells. Begin by getting very relaxed and closing your eyes. Use the following script as a guide, or record it on tape and listen as you play it back.

You are now getting smaller and smaller—smaller and smaller—until you become a point of consciousness. As this small point, you can travel wherever you want. Time no longer exists. You just are.

Now become aware of your big toe on your left foot. Go there now. You will begin and end your journey here. Look around you. What do you see? It may be dark at first, but soon you are accustomed to the darkness. Once you are, notice you are in a single cell. There are thousands of cells around you. Notice how each cell is very transparent, with hundreds of small particles floating around inside. Also, be aware that it is warm around you. As you travel, you will usually feel this same level of warmth. However, notice if there are any cool or hot spots as you travel, for this may signify an area of your body that needs attention. If so, you can later send healing energy to this part.

Now time to explore. Move on into your circulatory system and observe. The cells have a reddish tinge. It's a little like being in a red river, surrounded by walls. You see red and white platelets float by. Drop down into this river, and let it carry you along through your body. Whenever you want, you can leave this river to explore different parts of your body more closely. For now just move with the flow, and notice any warm and cool spots as you do.

Now travel up your left leg. Notice the ripples of your muscles, the whiteness and roundness of your bones and joints. Next travel on to your thigh and pelvic bones. Take a few moments to explore. Then on to your solar plexus and stomach area. Look around. Notice your diaphragm expanding up and down.

Next travel on to your heart. Observe its four chambers as you pass through. Your heart vibrates each time it pumps. Feel this vibration. Listen to it pulse. Then on to your chest and lungs. Notice how they expand and contract as the air rushes in and leaves. Explore your rib cage.

Now flow on to your left arm. Notice your muscles. Try flexing and releasing your arm. Observe how the muscles expand and contract. Then go down into your fingers. The walls of the blood vessels are smaller now. Explore your thumbs and fingers from the inside. Then return through your arm into your left shoulder. Notice the muscles and bones of your shoulders, and feel the power in the muscles.

Now travel on to your throat. As your vocal cords move, experience this vibration. Pay attention to your breath coming in and out of your windpipe. Next travel up the back of your neck, up your brain stem, and into your brain. Take some time to explore the intricate folds and patterns you find here. Then, suddenly, a thought speeds through your brain. Notice how it travels from nerve to nerve, as if along electric wires, and observe how one thought follows another. Next, feel your blood stream, pulsing through your brain.

Then, still in the center of your head, focus on the various parts of your body. From this position, you are an all-knowing manager and director. So ask yourself about the condition of your body. Are there any parts in your body that need attention? Is there anything you may have missed in your journey so far?

Then, when you are ready, begin your journey back down your right side. Again be aware of the warmth as you go. However, you can travel a little faster now, as you have already taken a quick look from the top.

So now, begin. Pass down through your neck into your shoulder. Then travel down your right arm, into your hand. Quickly explore your fingers. Come back up your arm. Now travel into your back. Slow down a little to explore your spine. Travel along the bumps and ridges. Feel its hardness. Notice how it bends.

Then travel back into your pelvic area and flow on into your right leg. Pass your thigh, your knee, down to your big toe, and then up your leg again, across your pelvis, and down into your left leg. Follow it downward now, back to your left big toe, where your journey began.

Now take a few moments to review your experience. Were there any places you noticed that seemed especially cool or hot? Any places that seemed to be weak or need some special attention? If so, note them, so you can later send them healing energy.

Finally, let your consciousness return to your head and expand from a small point of consciousness until you return to your normal waking state.

BREAKING BAD HABITS

The following techniques are based on the principle that you have to reprogram your mind to get rid of a habit because any habit becomes a pattern in your subconscious, and the behavior you want to change flows from this mental set. Therefore, when you reprogram yourself, you change this mental imprint to something you want, and your changed behavior flows naturally from this new pattern. Then, in time, this pattern becomes a habit, too, which is what you want.

As any habit is fixed in your unconscious, it takes some time to change your programming—about twenty-one days according to experts in this field. Thus, for any of these techniques to be effective, you must work with them for approximately three weeks until your new habit pattern has become automatic.

Until then, there is a lingering effect that keeps pushing you back to the habit you're trying to leave behind. For example, suppose you want to stop smoking, because your boss has said no more smoking in the office and you think it would be good for your health to stop anyway. Even if you stop cold, that longing for a cigarette may stay with you for several weeks, for it takes time to make your urge for old habits go away.

Your mind power, however, can give you the conviction you need to start the reprogramming process, and it can help speed up the process. It works in three ways: It helps you (1) decide if you really want to give up a habit; (2) develop a dislike for the habit, so you have the determination to change; and (3) see yourself the way you want to be with a new desirable behavior pattern replacing the habit you don't want.

---

1. HOW TO KNOW IF YOU REALLY WANT TO GIVE IT UP   Time: 1-2 minutes

The first step to giving up a habit is becoming clear that you really want to change. You may think you do, but possibly you may not. For instance, everyone in your office is giving up smoking, so you think you should, too. But in reality, smoking makes you feel easier when you are with people. It gives you a ritual, something to do. So down deep, you are not ready to give it up.

So how do you learn what you really want? Do you *really* want to stop that habit, whatever it is? Are you ready to stop it *now?* To find out, you can ask your body for cues to your inner wants.

One method is a variation of the full body yes-no pendulum technique for solving problems and making decisions as described in Chapter 12. As in the basic technique, stand straight, feet slightly apart, and visualize your body as a pendulum, which rocks forward and back to signify "yes," from right to left to signify "no," and in a circle to signify "maybe" or "not sure now." If you haven't used the basic technique, experiment a few times, using yes-no questions for which you know the answer, until your body responds appropriately to each question.

Now begin. In turn, ask three questions, and after each one, wait for your body to answer. These questions are: Do I really want to give up this habit? Am I ready to give it up now? Is it in my best interest to give it up? If all your answers are yes, work on getting rid of this habit. If not, better ask yourself why. (See the techniques for deciding what you want in Chapter 6.) There may be some good reasons why you aren't ready to give up your habit or why it is not in your best interest to do so.

2. LEARN TO HATE THAT HABIT   Time: 3-5 minutes

Assuming you're ready to give up your habit, the next stop is to make yourself really hate it with your whole being. To do this, imagine all the bad things you can about this habit and mentally experience one or more of them happening to you.

To begin, close your eyes and relax. Now see in your mind's eye the question: "What is bad about this habit?" and meditate on it for a few minutes. Let the thoughts pop into your mind. Don't try to analyze them or react. Just note each thought as it comes. Then, when the thoughts no longer come spontaneously, pick one of these bad qualities to experience.

Now, see yourself experiencing this bad quality as vividly as possible. For example, if your bad habit is smoking, and one of the worst problems for you is coughing, imagine that this is happening to you. See yourself cough and choke. And to make the experience even more intense, imagine that this problem is occurring in a public setting that creates an embarrassing situation for you. For instance, you are coughing at an important meeting or presentation, and everyone suddenly looks at you with concern.

After having this bad experience for a few minutes, counteract this negative image by pleasantly seeing yourself without the habit (as described in the next section), so you are left with a positive image, and don't end your techniques session feeling discouraged and depressed.

3. GOING, GOING, GONE   Time: 3-5 minutes

This technique is a continuation of 2, although you can use it by itself. However, combining the stick and carrot approach together (hating the habit and seeing yourself without it), is more effective than using the carrot alone.

The basic approach is simple. You see yourself as vividly as possible without the habit, and as a result, you reap all sorts of benefits—for instance, friends flock around you, people congratulate you, you gain a prize for your accomplishment. You pick your own rewards—what would be most valuable to you. The following scenario is one example:

Experience yourself without the habit. You feel happy, joyous. You have accomplished so much. You have worked hard and have gotten rid of your habit. So now see yourself celebrating. Your associates at work are honoring you with a big party. Everyone is laughing, singing. People come over and congratulate you. You feel very excited, pleased. Now someone comes over to you with a big box, wrapped brightly and tied with a ribbon. Excitedly, you open it and pull out a big trophy bearing the words: "Congratulations—You've Done It." Delightedly, you hold it up to show everyone, and you feel great.

 *Chapter 14*

Enrich Your Everyday Experiences

These mind power techniques can also be used to make your everyday experiences at work and elsewhere more interesting. You can use them to enliven a dull or routine task or make waiting time more creative. In turn, you'll feel more relaxed, energetic, and refreshed whatever you have to do, and will be more effective in getting jobs done.

For example, as a salesman, Bob J. spend a great deal of time on the road driving between prospects. To pass the time, he often listened to self-help and motivational tapes. But after listening to them for a few hours, he found he couldn't concentrate or take in any more information. Before he began using the mind power techniques, he often felt very restless and impatient during these quiet periods, and found himself counting the miles or thinking how long it would be to his destination. However, after he learned how to focus his mind on other things, he found he could use this time more productively; to solve problems, set goals, visualize himself performing some skill, or just entertain himself mentally.

Ann S. faced similar waiting or dead-time problems. Her job as a freelance writer and magazine columnist led her to set up many interviews, and often she had to wait for her interviewee, sometimes minutes to an hour. Frequently, she flipped through a magazine or newspaper as she waited. But many times, she didn't feel like reading what was there or there wasn't anything there to read. Then she found it relaxing and invigorating to go into her mind power frame of mind and use a few techniques to spur her energy and creativity. Also, she 157 often used these techniques while waiting in line for something such as in the supermarket, post office, and toll-booth plaza.

In short, these techniques are ideal to fill up dead time when you are involved in a repetitive task or between tasks. In turn, by using them, you'll find yourself more relaxed and energetic when you need to be back "on" again.

MAKE WAITING TIMES AND ROUTINE TASKS MORE INTERESTING

The following examples show how you can use your mind powers to make these waiting or dull times more useful and interesting. The first two exercises involve listening more closely to the sounds around you; the third requires looking more carefully at what you see; and the fourth helps you pay more attention to your sense of touch.

---

1. LISTENING WHILE YOU WORK   Time: 5-10 minutes

This is a way to spark up a routine task by listening closely to the sounds around you while you work. As long as the task doesn't require much conscious thought, such as stuffing envelopes, driving a truck, or working on an automatically controlled factory line, you can take a few minutes while you work to consciously listen. It's best to limit this exercise to five to ten minutes at a stretch, so you don't space out and then aren't ready to respond when you need to do so. But practiced for a short time, this exercise can stimulate you by varying the pace.

Start by telling yourself you are now going to do some active listening. Then, begin paying attention to the sounds around you.

First notice any sounds you are making as you perform your task. What is this sound like? Be aware of its quality. Is it heavy, sharp, continuous, jangly, soft, loud, or what? Is there any pattern or rhythm to this sound? How does it change over time? Just listen. Then, notice what other sounds are present. Shift your awareness from one sound to another. What happens as you do so? Next notice your own sounds as you move around—your breathing, your feet shuffling, your clothes rustling, and the like. Now be aware of several sounds at once. Variously shift your attention from one to another. Finally be aware of all the sounds as they blend into one.

2. TAKING TIME OUT TO LISTEN   Time: 5-10 minutes

When you have to wait for some time, you can avoid getting bored and impatient by calming yourself down and listening to the sounds you usually ignore.

It's a technique you can use anywhere. As appropriate, close your eyes to listen, or concentrate on some spot ahead of you with your eyes open. As in the previous exercise, limit the time you do this, so you don't get too spacey or fall asleep. However, if you have a fairly long waiting period, you can alternate this mind power technique with a few minutes of ordinary attention until your waiting is over.

To begin, tell yourself you are now going to do some active listening. Then, be silent and let your world quiet down. At first you may experience silence. But gradually, you will become aware of soft, unfamiliar, or distant sounds—such as the rustle of the wind, the flutter of a bird's wing, the purr of a motor. As these sounds appear, direct your attention in different directions, and project it near and far. See if you can focus in on specific sounds; then listen closely. Next, focus on two or more sounds at one time, or shift your attention from one sound to another. Notice how the sounds fade in and out.

3. SEEING FOR YOURSELF   Time: 2-3 minutes

To make a routine task more interesting or add variety to a waiting period, you can look at the world around you as a series of pictures. As you do, notice what each picture contains, as if you were seeing your world for the first time.

To begin, tell yourself you are now going to do some active seeing and will pay close attention to whatever you look at.

Then, imagine yourself as a photographer or picture framer. Now, as you look around, visualize a frame around what you see. Initially, if it helps, frame a scene with your thumbs and forefingers, and move your frame around to create different pictures. Later, you can dispense with this frame and create pictures with your imagination alone.

After you frame each picture, observe it closely. Notice its composition, the colors, the play of light and dark. Be aware if anything is moving through your picture. Now change the size of your frame. Make it larger, smaller. What do you see? Next create a moving picture by moving your frame. To create a zoom effect, move the frame toward you and away—just like in the movies.

4. TOUCHING AND SMELLING   Time: 3-5 minutes

Another way to make whatever you are doing—such as a routine work task or wait for something—more interesting, is to become aware of how the objects around you feel and of any smells around you. As this exercise involves touching things, make sure you are in a setting where you can do this freely, such as in a private office, alone in a waiting room, or in a crowd, where no one will pay special attention to you. Be prepared to stop should anyone interrupt you.

To begin, tell yourself that you are now going to pay special attention to whatever you touch or smell.

Then, start moving your hands slowly over all the objects around you. As you do, pay attention to their textures. If you can, close your eyes as you feel. Be aware of shapes, sizes, the changes from one texture to another. Notice how some are rough, some smooth; some shapes curve, others are sharp and angular. Some textures repeat themselves. Notice any bumps, ridges, depressions.

See if you can feel differences between different colors. The warmer colors (red, yellow, and orange) may feel warmer; the cooler colors (blue, purple, and green) cooler. Some objects may be harder or softer than others.

If you are near water, dip your hands in it or let it run over your hands. Hold your hands up and feel for air currents or differences in temperature.

You can also experiment with using other parts of your body besides your hands to feel. For example, try touching things with your elbows, nose, cheeks, lips, torso, and knees and notice what you experience.

Then, be aware of any smells. Ask yourself if any objects you have felt have a smell. Lift them to your nose, or bend down and move your face over them. Do you smell anything? Do you find any differences in smells as you move from one object to another? How would you characterize the quality of what you smell? Is something pungent? Sweet? Musky? Light? Heavy? What other words would you use?

EXPERIENCE EVERYDAY ACTIVITIES MORE FULLY

Besides making routine and waiting times more interesting, you can make other everyday experiences more vital, too. For instance, if you are taking a walk during lunch hour and enjoying your lunch in a park or restaurant, you can use your mind powers to have a more stimulating walk or lunch. You do this by becoming more aware of your feelings, surroundings, images, and thoughts wherever you are.

The following examples demonstrate some ways to do this. As you use these techniques, you'll find that every day becomes a more vibrant adventure, and you'll approach your work with more enthusiasm and energy, too.

---

1. EXPERIENTIAL WALK

You can take an experiential walk anywhere, anytime. Just walk and be open to look and perceive in new ways, such as the following:

As you walk, imagine you are someplace else — in another city, another time. Let the people, objects, and places you pass suggest other scenes or times. For instance, some wisps of fog around a street lamp may seem mystical or eerie, and suggest Victorian London or a village in France. Imagine yourself there as you walk.

Notice any shadows around you. Are they still? In motion? What odd shapes do they form? Maybe they look like someone or something else. Notice how your own shadow shifts as you walk.

Breathe in at different rates and observe your breathing. Notice any differences when you breathe fast or slow. Ask yourself how you feel. Then, as you breathe in and out, imagine that your breath is linking you to all people and things around you. Perhaps see your breath sending out and receiving little energy cords from everything and everyone. Think about how this feels, and notice what images appear.

As you pass people on your walk, create stories about who they are and what they are doing. For example, you might fantasize that an old woman with a bundle has recently arrived from abroad and has a strange story to tell; or perhaps that the business executive striding rapidly down the street is going to close an intriguing deal. Don't worry about the "truth." Make your fantasies as interesting and dramatic as you wish.

2. SCENIC PROJECTION

You can project yourself into an interesting scene wherever you are — while walking around, relaxing over lunch or cocktails, anywhere.

Look around, and with your eyes closed or open, imagine yourself walking through this area in your mind's eye. First, glance about to get a mental picture of the scene. Then, in your mind's eye, move about and explore. As you do, be aware of smells, sounds, textures, objects. Perhaps stop to touch and taste things. Imagine other people passing. Follow them if you like. Or if they are talking, listen to what they say. It's all in your imagination, so let your inhibitions go and do what you like. For example, if you want to go up to someone at a cocktail party and introduce yourself, do it. If you want to promote yourself to boss and fly off in your Lear Jet, do that, too.

3. PICTURE TRIPPING

For an alternate type of scenic projection, try imagining yourself in the pictures you see on the walls of an art gallery or office building. If you are looking through a book with pictures — such as a big coffee table book — while waiting to see someone, see yourself in the scene.

Begin by looking at the picture. Then, with your eyes open or closed, imagine yourself in the picture. If it is a realistic picture, walk around the scene. If an abstraction, move about from shape to shape or color to color. As you explore, pay attention to such things as: Who are you? How do you feel? What images and associations pop into your head? Does anything happen on your journey? Is anyone with you? Do they say anything? Do the objects or images in the picture have an interesting texture? How does this feel? And so on....

4. MAKING ASSOCIATIONS

This association technique is an enjoyable way to pass a lunchbreak, bus trip to or from work, or any time when you have a few minutes alone to sit and relax. You probably remember seeing pictures in a cloud as a child. It was a time to relax, experiment, and enjoy creating new images and experiences. Now this technique helps you see pictures and associations everywhere.

Begin by sitting quietly for a few minutes wherever you are. Then, look around and focus on various parts of your environment in turn. As you do, notice what images and associations emerge. For example, a rock may look like a man's face; a knarled tree may suggest a wild animal; a park bench may remind you of the entrance to an underground cave filled with treasures. Wherever you look, pause for a few moments and see what images and responses come.

 *Chapter 15*

Use the Power of Your Mind to Get Away From It All

The final way these mind power techniques can help you with your work or business is by giving you a form of mental release at times when you need to pull away from your work situation to unwind but don't have the time to take a vacation. I frequently use these techniques this way myself, when I have many deadlines and can't get away. But instead, for a short time, I can escape and take a trip with my mind. Then, I return to whatever I am doing feeling refreshed and ready to go again.

In a way, this approach is much like daydreaming. But it is a more organized, intense, focused experience. Thus, I find it increases my energy and leaves me feeling ready to go again, whereas I feel a little scattered and lethargic after ordinary daydreaming.

There are two major forms of mind tripping I recommend. One is listening to music with all your senses, so the music becomes a more intense and vivid experience. The other is taking a mental trip to another place, essentially creating a movie in your mind.

EXPERIENCE MUSIC MORE INTENSELY

The way to experience any kind of music—classical, pop, rock, whatever you like—more intensely is to activate your other senses, so you not 163 only hear the music, but see it, feel it, perhaps move with it. These techniques give you this more vivid enjoyable, uplifting experiencing because they stimulate your senses in three main ways.

- They stimulate your visual sense, so you see different imagery as you listen.

- They make you more aware of your bodily responses to the music and the feelings that result.

- They make you more sensitive to your physical movements, so they expand your kinesthetic sense.

Furthermore, these techniques encourage the development of synesthesia—or a blending of the senses, so you experience the sensations simultaneously and therefore more intensely in several sensual modes. It's a little like going to the movies and seeing a 70mm film played with speakers around the room.

USING YOUR VISUAL SENSE TO EXPERIENCE MUSIC
MORE FULLY   Time: 5-30 minutes

The following techniques are designed to help you to have a more intense, enjoyable musical experience by using your visual abilities to see images as you listen.

1. Create a Musical Scene. *Create a scene as you listen to music. Sit, lie down, or move about as you listen. Close your eyes if you wish. As you listen, let an image of a place come to mind. Don't force it. Just let it come. Then look around the scene. Explore. Observe the landscape, notice if any people are there. If so, watch them move with the music. Let the scene unfold, like a music-inspired movie in your mind. Perhaps create a story by letting it emerge as you listen. The music will suggest images and story ideas.*

2. See How Sound Affects the Sun. *Observe how the sounds of music affect the rays of light from the sun. To do this, listen to music on a sunny day. Close your eyes and look toward the sunlight. Notice that the darkness is filled with sparkling flickers of light—the sun's rays filtering through your closed lids. As the music plays, watch these light sparkles dance and vibrate with the music.*

3. Form a Musical Sculpture. *Become aware of how the music creates a sound sculpture of three-dimensional space. To begin, close your eyes, and imagine the music is like a sculptor shaping your body with its touch. Notice that the notes hit different parts of your body, tracing an outline of your body's shape. Then, notice how all the sounds have a position in space, so that the music can create sculptures around you. Look carefully and see various forms emerge, expressing the music. For example, if the music is gentle and soft, you might see undulating, rolling forms. If it*

is staccato and jangling, perhaps you might see angular shapes, like icicles hanging in space. Just listen, and see what shapes appear.

4. Design a Musical Landscape. *Let the music create a landscape in your mind. Start by imagining a ball or dot in front of your eyes. As you watch, the ball goes up and down in response to the music's rhythm and tone. Also, it moves closer or further away as the music grows loud and soft. So as the music plays, the moving ball creates a three-dimensional spatial relief map or landscape, reflecting the music. It may have valleys, mountains, rivers, other features—all carved out by the ball as it moves. Once the landscape is completed, let the ball drop out, and then, in your mind's eye, walk into this landscape and explore it.*

5. Choreograph a Dance. *Create a dance in your mind's eye. First visualize a stage or screen in your mind. Soon some characters in colorful costumes appear and begin to dance. Notice their steps and how they move. They may leap, twirl, do flips. Several dancers may form into a circle or line. They may toss each other in the air. Perhaps their dance tells a story. Let the story line emerge as you watch. Once the scene is set, you can imagine yourself joining the dance in your mind'e eye; or perhaps start to dance in reality, with the scene or story you have created in mind.*

6. How Music Creates Motion. *Observe the music's vibrations by watching a candle burn. To prepare, get a candle and light it in a dark room. Then, as the music plays, look at the flame. Watch it move in response to the music. Imagine the flame and music as one. Now observe the candle closely—look at its texture, color, the pattern of the wax as it burns. Finally, place your hands one over the other to create a matrix with your fingers, hold them in front of your eyes, and move them back and forth as you listen and watch the flame. You'll create an interesting strobe effect.*

EXPERIENCING THE MUSIC MORE INTENSELY THROUGH YOUR BODILY SENSATIONS AND FEELINGS   Time: 5-30 minutes

The next set of exercises will help you have a more intense, relaxing musical experience by showing you how to pay more attention to your bodily sensations, as your body reacts to the vibrations of the music. As you listen, you'll notice a wide range of sensations. For instance, depending on what it is, the music can feel like a caress or a drum beat; a sharp charge of energy or a feathery stroke. In turn, these sensations can help you relax or feel charged up, ecstatic, and ready to go. The following techniques are designed to give you various types of feeling experiences.

1. Find Your Musical Target. *Experience musical vibrations focused in different parts of your body. By holding an object, like a coin, watch, or pendant, against these areas as you concentrate, you can intensify the feeling there.*

To begin, assume any comfortable position (sitting, standing, lying down), and feel free to move about if you wish. Then relax and listen. Note the different tones and pitches, and notice how their vibrations stimulate different body areas—the lower ones resonate through your pelvis and abdominal areas; the higher ones vibrate around your throat, forehead, or top of your head. This occurs because different pitches activate different energy centers.

Now concentrate on receiving the musical vibrations in specific parts of your body—a knee, an elbow, a thigh, your stomach, your heart, your throat. Try holding an object where you want to focus the vibrations. Notice the differences if you alternately hold this object there and take it away. Usually, the vibrations intensify where you hold it.

Then experiment. Try holding two objects at different spots. Alternately focus on one spot and then the other, or visualize energy flowing from one spot to another. As you focus on different body parts, try experimenting with different body positions— such as standing, sitting, lying down, curling up, or lifting your legs above your head. And notice the different sensations when you change the way you sit, lie, or stand.

2. Feel the Energy Flow. *Experience the musical vibrations flowing like energy through your body.*

To begin, stand or sit upright. With your eyes closed, relax and listen for a few minutes. Then imagine the musical vibrations are a beam of energy coming up through your feet. Feel this beam travel up your spine, spread through your body, and flow out through your head. As the energy flows up, lift your arms, and let it flow out through them. Then turn off this energy flow.

Next, see this musical energy beam come down through your head. Feel the beam travel down your spine, flow into your feet, and into the earth. Compare any differences you experience when the energy flows down versus when it flows up. Then turn off this energy.

Now feel the music flow up and down at the same time. Notice any differences from your previous experiences. Then turn off this energy, too.

Finally, let the music come in through your hands. Hold out your hands, and imagine the music flowing into your hands and down through your body. Again pay attention to your feelings and note any differences from your previous experiences. Then, when ready, turn off this energy and return to normal consciousness.

3. Change Your Form. *Experience the music differently as you imagine your body in a different form. To begin, assume any position, and feel free to move about. First, just listen and feel the music flow through you. Then, while you listen, imagine your body changing its form. Note how this feels and how it affects the way you move. For example, you might imagine your body is a different substance, like a rock, a piece of metal, or the wind. Or imagine yourself an animal, like a cat, lion, rabbit, or snake. Or think of your body changing in size or weight and experience how this feels.*

4. Try the Musical Hit. *Raise your energy and stimulate imagery by slapping different body areas as you listen. As usual, relax and close your eyes. Then, beginning with your lower legs, slap your body vigorously with your hands. Then move up to your knees, thighs, pelvic area, and on to your stomach and waist. Next go on to your chest and back, and finally on to your head. As you slap each area, be aware of your feelings and any images and thoughts.*

BECOMING MORE SENSITIVE TO YOUR PHYSICAL MOVEMENTS THROUGH IMAGERY

The next two techniques will help you experience music more intensely while you move to it. For example, when you sway or dance to music and combine this movement with imagery, this intensifies your experience of the music. Then, when the experience is over and you're ready to return to the everyday world, you feel charged up and ready to go.

---

1. IMAGE AND SOUND

Use imagery to intensify your movements to music as you exercise or dance. Some possible images to use as you move are the following, or create your own images.

- *Imagine you are in a different place (like a cave, mountain top, or underwater) and move accordingly.*
- *Imagine you are a color and move as this color.*
- *Imagine you are one of the elements (earth, air, fire, or water).*
- *Imagine you are an object, plant, or animal.*
- *Imagine you are a marionette on a string.*
- *Imagine you are being blown by the wind.*
- *Imagine that the music is like a sculptor, who shapes you and moves you around.*
- *Let the music massage your body, and notice how this feels.*
- *Imagine the music is alternately far away and near. Notice how it gets softer and louder as your perceptions change.*
- *Visualize the air in front of you as a large ball of energy. Notice that you can push against it or move it around in various ways. You can lift it, push it down, squeeze it together, shove it away, throw it to someone, shift it from hand to hand, bounce it like a ball.*

2. DANCE SCENARIO

Combine a series of images together, and use them as a guide while you dance or exercise. You can use the following scenario as a sample. Think about it or perhaps record it on tape and play it back as you move.

First, imagine that your consciousness is located outside you somewhere in the room. Project it outward, so you can look back on yourself as you dance.

Now shift your consciousness from one part of the room to another, and look back at yourself. Be aware of how you look from different positions.

Now project your consciousness to different parts of your body, such as your feet and hands. Try looking at yourself from here.

Next, imagine you are focusing your energy on different parts of your body, and experiment with moving that part. For example, send energy to your hand and move your hand. Send it to your feet and move your feet.

Now rub your hands together. Pull them apart slowly and feel the energy between them. See how far apart you can move them and still feel the energy.

Now move your hands around this energy. Touch it. Feel it. Imagine it a piece of clay, and shape it into some form. Next push this energy with your hands. Move it up and down, from left to right.

Now let your whole body be a sculptor, and as you dance, press against and mold the energy with your hands, your feet, your whole body. Then rub your body with the energy around you, as if taking a shower or bath.

Now see yourself as an animal, and move as it does. Make animal noises.

Finally, choose to be an object and move like that.

TAKE A MENTAL JOURNEY AND GET A QUICK SURGE OF EXCITEMENT

Taking a mental journey is an excellent way to gain a quick and refreshing charge of excitement by going on an adventure in your mind. Like a moving picture screen, your mind can take you wherever you want. Or perhaps think of the experience as a mini-vacation for your mind that you can use for various purposes. For instance, use it to enjoy a brief glimpse of your personal fantasy world or vicariously experience things you would otherwise fear, like daredevil sports and edge-of-the-seat adventures to exotic places. You can go back in time to visit historical spots that fascinate you, voyage to outer space, maybe project yourself into an imaginary future.

Unlike a daydream, you don't simply let your mind drift in this journey. Instead, you have a general plan or map to guide you. Then, as you travel along this path, you notice and observe carefully, so that the experience becomes especially real. Afterwards, return to the everyday world feeling invigorated and renewed.

Feel free to create your own mental itineraries. The following four guides are designed to get you started and give you a model for creating your own adventure.

These guidelines can be used in three ways.

- Read the trip and use it as a flexible guide for your own experience.
- Record the trip on tape, then play it back and let it guide you.
- Get together with a friend or group. Have one person read the journey while the rest experience it.

In all of these trips, the basic approach is the same. You get comfortable, relax, and make your mind a big blank movie screen. Then for fifteen to thirty minutes, you let the images flow.

These four sample voyages will take you to outer space, to a past or future time, on an underwater adventure, and on a parachute descent. Following these, other possibilities are listed. The trips you can take are infinite.

---

1. BLAST OFF FOR A JOURNEY TO OUTER SPACE   Time: 15-30 minutes

You are a passenger in a space capsule, voyaging far beyond our galaxy, to an intergalactic space community on a far away planet. It is the year 3000.

Now enter the space ship. Go directly to your life support capsule. It is very comfortable inside and you can relax completely, as you travel quickly from one end of the universe to another. Now feel the ship sway slightly as it blasts off from planet earth. As it does, look out of the small window next to your capsule, and see the earth falling away below you. Soon it begins to look like a small ball, with patches of green and blue representing the continents and the oceans.

Glance about and notice the vast black expanse of space before you, although here and there you see clusters of stars twinkling brightly. You feel awed by this grand beauty, and the silence of space gives you a sense of wonder and peace. All you can hear is the whirr of your own space ship, and beyond only silence everywhere.

Now, to experience the weightlessness of space, put on your space suit and leave your life support capsule for a few minutes. Attach your life line and open the hatch. As you step out into space, feel yourself floating. You feel absolutely weightless, suspended on a vast inky sea, filled with sparkling white dots.

Now time to return to your ship. Your destination is approaching fast, for while you have been floating, your ship has been hurtling quickly through hundreds and thousands of miles—so fast and smoothly you haven't even noticed. So get back into your life support capsule, as your ship comes to the end of your journey.

Now notice a large planet before you. It is made up of grey granite rocks and soil; and you can see jagged crags and wide plateaus rising above the surface. On one of these plateaus, you notice a long white air strip. Your space ship is heading towards this. As the ship comes closer, it slows down, until finally it lands gently on the center of the strip.

Go to the hatchway, push it open, and step out. After you comes the captain of the ship, who you haven't seen before. He is tall, rugged-looking, wearing a white space suit, like you. He motions to you to tell you it is safe to explore wherever you want. So you wander off feeling safe, confident, and eager to explore.

You begin by approaching an unusual rock formation that intrigues you. It is tall, shaped like a lightening bolt, and you make a circuit around it.

Then, as you walk on, you pass small lichen-like plants clinging to the rocks. Pick one up. It looks soft, mossy, fragile.

Next, you pass a few odd shaped boulders. They are round, but with a series of ridges and projections. Strangely, they feel light when you lift them. When you drop them, they bounce slightly a few times.

After a while, you approach the outskirts of a civilization or settlement. There are a few houses, buildings, and free-standing walls. However, they are different from any structures you have seen on earth, as a series of projections jut out from each surface. Curious, you go over and explore these closely. Some more moss clings to the walls. Also, you notice some unusual greenish-yellow plants, with large leaves, like elephant ears.

Then, in the distance, you notice a few people riding toward you in an open jeep-like vehicle. There are three of them, and they appear very different from people on earth. They have large round heads, small eyes, long gangly arms. They wear silvery metallic suits. But they seem friendly. As they pull up towards you, they motion you over and offer you a ride to see their city.

You get in, and, as you drive, they tell you about some of their customs—what their family life is like, about their government, how they make a living. Listen as they describe their way of life.

Now you enter their city center. It is made up of large domed houses made from strange white rocks with long projections. The small domes are private houses; the larger ones apartments; the very biggest, government and cultural buildings. Take some time to explore. You can visit some people in their homes if you like, and see how they live.

Now you hear a loud whine coming from the vehicle. Your hosts are motioning to you. It's time to go back to your ship. You return to their vehicle, and they drive you back. There you shake hands to say goodbye and reenter your ship. Inside you get back in your life support capsule, take off your space suit, and drift off to sleep. Now many dreams and images come to you about the planet you have seen. When you awake, your ship is landing on planet Earth again. Refreshed, you get up and step out. Once again you are home.

On a subsequent trip, create your own planetary world and space beings.

2. TAKE A VOYAGE THROUGH TIME   Time: 15-30 minutes

You are standing at the door of a large laboratory that contains a time machine that can take you through time and space to wherever you want to go. The laboratory is a large concrete building, standing in the middle of a desert. All around you are miles and miles of sand. You knock on the door, and soon a white-coated scientist opens the door and ushers you in.

The scientist leads you down a long corridor and into a small room. Directly in front of you is a control panel with many knobs, levers, and dials. At the scientist's direction, you sit down at this panel, and he draws a curtain behind you. He explains that this time machine will take you back and forward in time to any place you choose.

Now the scientist points to some buttons with numbers. As he explains, you press these to indicate the date you want to go to, turn a dial to indicate the place, and press down a large lever. He explains that when you open the curtain and walk out of the laboratory, you will be at your destination. You nod to indicate you understand, and the scientist leaves, closing the curtain behind him.

You turn to the controls, trying to decide where you want to go. You think for a few moments, and decide on the age of Napoleon in France. To get there, you maneuver the buttons and dials to select the date and place, then press the lever. At once, there is a loud whirring sound, and the whole room seems to shake and rumble, although your chair remains perfectly still. A red light flashes "on." The whirr gets louder; some white lights flash; and the shaking continues, although your chair doesn't move. Then, finally, the motion stops; the flashing lights go off; the whirr stops. The room is quiet and still again. You wonder what has happened. You go over to the curtain and open it. In front of you, you see the long laboratory corridor, but no one is there. Its white halls gleam from the reflection of the bright sunlight outside.

Curious, you walk down the corridor, open the door, and step out into the sunlight. But it looks different from when you entered—for you are in a different time and place—in France, during Napoleon's reign. But no one can see you, because you are invisible.

Now look around. You are in the country on a country road. Around you, fertile farms spread out like patchwork quilts, and peasants bustle about. The women wear long dark skirts, with kerchiefs around their heads, and the men wear big wide pantaloons and large scarves. They are doing various farm chores—feeding the chickens, threshing grain, bundling hay.

Then, suddenly, down the road, you hear the sounds of a festival. Drums, pipes, singing, laughter. The peasants look up from their chores and quickly finish. Soon they hurry down the road to join the festivities, and you follow them.

It's a parade. The officials of the town are gathered at one side of the road, dressed in their best finery: long black coats, military uniforms, cloaks. Near them stand their wives, wearing long white dresses. Some hold lacy parasols. Now a coach drawn by four white horses appears. Surrounding it are a guard of military men in sharp blue uniforms seated on sleek white horses. Inside the coach in the darkness you can just make out Napoleon, dressed in full military regalia—a bright red jacket, with dozens of sparkling military medals on his left side. After the coach comes a platoon of drummers, clicking their sticks on their drums as they march. As the coach passes, the peasants cheer, wave handkerchiefs, throw flowers, and bow deeply. Napoleon waves his handkerchief from the window and nods in recognition as he passes.

After the parade, you follow a peasant back to his house to observe everyday life in this era. His wife makes dinner and serves it in a large wooden bowl. She brings it over to the heavy wooden table in the center of the kitchen, where the peasant and a half dozen children of various ages are sitting. They fill their plates full and eat greedily. After dinner, when it gets dark, the peasant lights a candle, pulls out his fiddle, and everyone joins in an exuberant medley of songs.

Now it's time to return. Go back to the road and walk back to where you came from. After you walk a ways, notice a large mound of dirt to your right, and go over to it. To one side, you see a small door. Open it and go in. It leads back into the laboratory. Follow the long corridor to another door, and open it. Now you are back on the desert again.

On subsequent trips, pick other places and times and imagine what they might be like. Don't worry about accuracy. Remember this is a fantasy journey so you can get away from it all. However, if you have been to an unfamiliar place and are curious, you can check out the details for accuracy. If you are correct, there may be several explanations—choose the one that makes the most sense to you:

• you have some psychic ability and are picking up the information psychically;

• the trip has triggered a reincarnation experience;

• you were a good history student and have remembered your lessons well.

A few other popular trips might be to:

• ancient Egypt
• ancient Greece or Rome
• medieval Europe
• the American frontier
• early Christian times
• the Italian Renaissance
• the Stone Age
• you name it!

3. HAVE AN UNDERWATER ADVENTURE   Time: 15-30 minutes

You are standing beside a beautiful seashore. You may have been there before or maybe not. As far as you can see, there is only blue sky, blue sea, and white sand.

Listen to the waves. They lap softly on the beach. They seem gentle, welcoming. As you take a deep breath in and exhale, notice you are breathing in harmony with the movement of the tide.

Now put on your diving gear. There is a light on your mask, so you can see wherever you go. Spray on your special shark and fish repellent. This will keep you perfectly safe, so nothing will bother you.

Now dive into the water. Notice how natural it seems for you. Feel how calm you become as your body moves with the water. You feel light, buoyant. Watch the bubbles rise to the surface as you go deeper and deeper into the sea. Watch the light as it plays on the moving water. Your vision underwater is clear and perfect.

Look around you. Schools of fish swim by, flowing with the current. They create a kaleidoscope of colors, some polka-dotted, some striped. They flash by, as if lit by neon. There are so many of them. You see them coming from all directions, moving constantly, and darting in and out. It's like watching colorful splashes of paint dance by.

Now it's time to descend further. Below you see a sunken ship, partially covered with sand. You climb around it to get a close-up view. It looks old, weathered, a little like a pirate ship. Perhaps there is a treasure chest aboard.

You swim down to look around. Inside, you notice the ship's fine carpentry and wood carvings, and you ask yourself: Where did this ship come from? Did it carry treasures across the world? Is there gold in here? If so, it may be in the captain's quarters.

The door ahead of you may lead there. You give a quick pull to open it; then swim away to let the mud and sand settle. Now you swim back to the doorway and go in. There is a log sitting on the desk, and you look at it. Although it has been faded and damaged by the water and time, you can still make out names, dates, and events. Take a few moments to read what you can.

Then, off to your right, you see a chest that may contain the treasure and nearby a silver key. Eagerly, you go to the chest and attempt to open it. But it's locked, so try the key. Good, it fits. So unlock the chest.

When you do, you discover that, yes, it is a treasure chest, filled with a fabulous treasure. Golden coins. Rings. Pottery, Jewels. A crown of fine gems. Golden statues. Robes of velvet and satin. Truly a priceless find. Take time to examine this treasure. See if you can identify where it comes from, what culture created these pieces. Look at the details. Feel the textures. Note the size and shapes of the art objects you see.

Now time to go on and see what else there is to discover underwater. Swim away from the ship, and watch the passing fish as you swim. You see sparkles of light flashing through the water as they pass. Notice how light and free you feel as you swim. You are flowing, drifting, feeling buoyed up by the water.

Then, as you move on, be aware of the various plants that inhabit the sea. Observe the crustaceans on the ocean floor. See how many forms of life you can observe.

Soon, you see up ahead an opening to a cave. It's just a small slit in the underwater rocks, and it looks inviting. So you swim toward it, curious to know what's inside. Could some interesting sea creatures live inside? Or maybe this cave was once above the sea, and the remains of another culture are here.

You swim in and find yourself in a long tunnel through the rocks. Your light allows you to see all around. As you move down the tunnel, you notice mysterious symbols on the walls, perhaps from a prehistoric age. At the end, you enter a large room. It seems to be lit by some strange, eerie glow from the phosphorous that gives off a shimmering colored light. It looks like the reflection of colored glass.

Now you take some time to explore around. You see giant shells everywhere. Then, in a far corner, you notice some exquisite treasures from an earlier people— delicately crafted golden mirrors, strands of exotic beads, golden baubles, silver necklaces. You can pick them up and look at them more closely.

Then, when you are ready to return, swim out of the cove and back to the shore.

4. PARACHUTE THROUGH SPACE

In a few minutes, you will execute a perfect parachute jump. Now you are in a small plane, which has taken off and is flying towards a large open field on a bright, sunny day. You are wearing a parachute on your back, and have a reserve chute across your stomach. Before boarding, your equipment was thoroughly checked and is in perfect condition. You are dressed warmly, in a down ski jacket and will be perfectly comfortable during your descent. Another parachutist, similarly dressed, is with you.

As the plane climbs into the sky, prepare to jump. It is a perfect day, almost cloudless, warm, and still. Look down through the window of the plane. You are flying over a plain now—below you see fields, a farmhouse here and there, cows and sheep grazing. The farmlands appear like a colored patchwork quilt. The earth looks soft and inviting. Just perfect for a jump.

Meanwhile, the plane has been climbing higher and the air is cooler. It feels refreshing, vitalizing. You feel energetic, excited, looking forward to your jump.

Now the plane levels off and begins to cruise. The other parachutist rises and goes to the door to jump first. For a few moments, he stands there poised, and then gracefully jumps. As he floats down, he moves his arms and legs around effortlessly. You can feel his sense of freedom and ease. Watch him become smaller as he floats down towards earth, and as he lands his parachute billows out.

Now your turn to jump. Stand at the doorway of the plane, and when you're ready, jump. As you do, experience the air around you. Feel its coolness against your cheeks. Notice that you are plummetting downward through space. You feel completely free.

Now be aware of the earth coming closer and closer. Watch the tiny farmhouses become larger. Notice how the patchwork of the fields and the highway lines becomes more detailed as you float down. You can even see a tiny car here and there. Be aware of how your perception changes. Notice wisps of clouds around you.

If you feel lively, try some games in the sky. Do a backflip, a somersault, whatever you want, and feel perfectly safe.

As you move closer to earth over an open field, prepare to pull your chute cord. Your chute billows out behind you, and you feel the pull as it slows your descent. Float for a while this way.

Then notice how close you are coming to earth. Closer. Closer. You feel excitement as you get closer. The earth comes toward you more quickly. Closer. Closer. Now extend your legs. You are ready to land. And you make a perfect landing on your feet.

Then when you are ready, return to normal consciousness and open your eyes.

On subsequent trips, you can try other exciting sports. Even if you wouldn't do it in reality, you can experience it now. For example, try a fling with:

- hang gliding
- downhill racing
- sports car racing
- skateboarding
- figure skating (like a champion, of course)
- going on a jungle safari
- you name it!

 *Chapter 16*

Making Mind Power Techniques a Regular Part of Your Life

The previous chapters have described a variety of mind power techniques you can use to help in your work and business and in other aspects of your life.

Each chapter has featured specific techniques for particular purposes. Also, I have tried to emphasize the principles underlying the use of these techniques to show that these can be modified and adapted, depending on your own situation, personality, behavioral style, previous experiences, and other factors. For everyone is different and has different goals, everyday challenges, and different systems of meaning. So if you would prefer to use another image or procedure to achieve a desired result, by all means, change it.

As long as you follow the basic principles and use these techniques fairly regularly (about twenty minutes or more a day), these techniques will work. The key is learning to relax, directing your mind power abilities to some goal, being confident you have the power to achieve what you want, and then letting your intuitive powers operate freely, so they are not restricted or held back by your logical mind. The techniques and images described in this book are designed to channel and guide this power. Then, once you create the open channel, your mind powers do the work.

Thus, no matter what you want to achieve in your work or business, no matter how you seek to enrich your life, you can direct your mind powers to achieve your goals. Just concentrate on creating what you want to happen, and soon you'll find that it will occur or that your work and life situation generally will change in positive ways.

Just watch. Positive things will begin to happen more frequently in your workplace and at home. Even if you don't ask for these things specifically, they will come, because working with your mind power abilities releases streams of constructive, positive energy, and when you mobilize your inner forces in this positive way, that's what you will get back.

To help you notice the change, keep a list of the goals you have achieved, or perhaps keep a regular journal to chart each day. In turn, keeping this list or journal will make the things you want happen even faster, as the act of keeping a list or journal makes you more open and aware.

In short, when you work on applying these mind power techniques, you'll change your work situation and life for the better. Decide what you want, and start the processes described in this book to get it.

And now...begin. You have the mind power abilities within you to mold and shape whatever you want!

For information on Mind Power workshops, seminars, and training programs, you can contact Gini Graham Scott in care of Creative Communications and Research, 308 Spruce Street, San Francisco, California, 94118, (415) 567-2747.

INDEX